Solomon Was a Businessman

Solomon Was a Businessman

Advice from the Wealthiest Man on Earth

ARDITH BAKER
DAVID WESLEY WHITLOCK

RESOURCE *Publications* · Eugene, Oregon

SOLOMON WAS A BUSINESSMAN
Advice from the Wealthiest Man on Earth

Resource Publications
A Division of Wipf and Stock Publishers
199 W. 8th Ave., Suite 3
Eugene, OR 97401

ISBN 13: 978-1-55635-989-7

Manufactured in the U.S.A.

Contents

Acknowledgments

Special thanks are expressed to our copyeditor, Dr. Linda Gray, for her assistance, and to the staff at Wipf and Stock, Resource Publications. Thanks to all our colleagues who contributed to this volume, and especially Marshal Wright, Walter MacMillan, Gordon Dutile, and C. Pat Taylor. Thanks to Steve Quinnelly and David Dyson for their inspiration and challenge to look deeper into the Word of God. We also express our appreciation to our spouses, Paul Baker and Dana Leigh Whitlock.

Introduction

Wisdom from the Proverbs

SOLOMON, THE king of Israel and son of Israel's greatest
King—David—was asked by Jehovah what he desired most.
His answer was "wisdom." Though God also granted Solomon
great wealth and power, the greatest gift was the answer to his
prayer. Inspired by the Holy Spirit, Solomon recorded many of
his sayings, and these wisdom verses are included in the book
of Proverbs

> *For attaining wisdom and discipline;*
> *for understanding words of insight;*
> *for acquiring a disciplined and prudent life,*
> *doing what is right and just and fair;*
> *for giving prudence to the simple,*
> *knowledge and discretion to the young.*
> (Prov. 1:2–4)

A wise pastor once counseled me to read one chapter of
Proverbs a day—one chapter for each day of the month, starting
over each month. Reading through these passages, I am struck
with how relevant and timely the proverbs are, not only for our
personal lives, but for our professional business lives as well. My
pastor knew that I would be blessed if I applied God's words of
wisdom to my daily living and my relationships.

Imagine, then, how our businesses might be blessed and
prosperous if we simply apply these truths to our business relationships as well! Like my pastor encouraged me, I also encour-

age you to read one chapter of Proverbs a day so that God can speak to you through his scripture. It is my greatest desire that God bless you and your business as you read and apply these scriptural truths.

—Ardith Baker

The Beginning of Knowledge

ARDITH BAKER

"The fear of the Lord is the beginning of knowledge,
but fools despise wisdom and discipline."

(Prov. 1:7)

FROM BIRTH until death, we acquire a vast amount of knowledge. In business, we depend upon knowledge to make sound business decisions, to get ahead of our competitors, to remain on the cutting edge, and ultimately to succeed. However, knowledge without divine insight and direction is just useless information. Solomon begins his book of Proverbs by setting the record straight. Recognizing the source of his knowledge and wisdom, he sums it up in this statement: "The fear of the Lord is the beginning of knowledge. . . ." Fearing God means that you acknowledge him as your creator and heavenly Father and submit to his will in your personal and business lives. This type of respect and submission is the first step toward true knowledge. Once this is established, your priorities straighten out and everything else—your relationships, finances, business—falls into place. Establish your knowledge base by acknowledging God. Make it your priority to increase your knowledge of him through prayer and his written Word. Respect his desire to love, guide, and direct you in all that you do. Then you will be able to go out in the world with this secure knowledge base, build on it, and succeed.

Thank you, Lord, for loving us and giving us the opportunity to learn and increase our knowledge. Give us insight and discretion so that we will apply our knowledge according to your wisdom and thus glorify your name. Amen.

3

Make All You Can

David Dyson

"Such is the end of all who go after ill-gotten gain;
it takes away the lives of those who get it."

(Prov. 1:19)

JOHN WESLEY, the Methodist missionary who evangelized England and America, challenged his audience to "make all you can." His challenge was not one motivated by greed, but encouraged stewardship of our time and resources. We are accountable for the talents and resources that have been entrusted to us as illustrated by the parable of the talents (Matt. 25:14–30). Reminders of the power of greed echo in our ears with the scenarios of Enron, TYCO, Global Crossing, and WorldCom and the stories of Ken Lay, Bernie Ebbers, Ivan Boesky, and Michael Milken. Proverbs 1:19 warns of the perils of the greedy; they will lose their very lives. Where, then, is the balance between "make all you can" and "greed"? Jesus' parables depict life as it should or should not be lived. Consider S. Truett Cathy, the founder of Chick-fil-A, as one example of the imitate-me-as-I-imitate-Christ scenario. Raised in a dysfunctional family, Cathy was never afforded a college education, yet his company has provided over $16 million in college scholarships. Cathy is the adopted "Grandpa" of hundreds of foster children. His quest to "make all you can" has been empowered by his generosity and is reflected in his company's purpose statement: "To glorify God by being faithful stewards of all that is entrusted to us." Wesley made two additional comments to complement his assertion to "make all you can." He also challenged his audience to "save all you can" and "give all you can."

4

Lord, you have given us the means to prosper and you even desire that we prosper and be in health (3 John 1:2). By your Spirit, give us wisdom to discern between greed and responsibility. Prosper us so that we have plenty to give. Amen.

Success and Significance

BRETT ANDREWS

*"When you grab all you can get, that's what happens:
the more you get, the less you are."*
(Prov. 1:19 MSG)

MANY POPULAR books have been written over the years about achieving success. Some of these books even begin to explore the relationship between success and significance. As a businessperson, I want to challenge you to critically examine your own definition of success. Is your definition God-inspired or world-related? Do you seek the accumulation of things, or do you actively seek the achievement of God's will in your life? If you're like me, you'll find that these are hard questions to ask about yourself because you know what the answers are: being guilty of listening too closely to the world's definition of success. With the advent of modern marketing research technology, it is all too easy for professional marketers to target you and me with specific advertisements that appeal directly to our specific desires for worldly items, thus providing us with a nonstop parade of temptations innocently disguised as product promotions. However, the Word advises us to temper the desire to accumulate material wealth by throwing ourselves into a relationship with Christ. Only through him can we avoid diminishing who we truly are and move from worldly success to eternal significance.

Lord, please help me to define myself and my success according to your definitions and not those of the world. Please allow my life at work to be an example of your life-changing power.

Wisdom, Knowledge, and Decision-Making

Marshal H. Wright

*"I would have poured out my heart to you
and made my thoughts known to you."*

(Prov. 1:23b)

PROVERBS 1 addresses the relationship among wisdom, knowledge, and the decisions we make in our day-to-day lives. This connection is critical for business leaders who are required to make strategic decisions for their organizations. One approach to decision-making, known as the "bounded-rationality approach," models the process as a "systematic analysis of a problem followed by choice and implementation," but where decisions are made "under severe time and resource constraints."[1] Proponents of this model assert that business executives are often required to resort to "intuitive" decision-making for the organization in the face of highly constrained and pressured (i.e., bounded) environments where the rational decision-making approach cannot be completely implemented. This is where the thoughts about wisdom found in Proverbs 1:23 really become relevant for the Christian business leader. Regardless of the time and resource constraints that we face, we have the assurance that if we truly seek the Lord, he will provide us with all of the wisdom and knowledge that we need to make wise decisions in all that we do.

Lord, I realize that in this ever-changing and fast-paced world, I do not, on my own, have the wisdom or knowledge to consistently

1. Richard L. Daft, *Organization Theory and Design*, 7th ed. (Cincinnati: South-Western College Publishing, 2001), 402.

make wise decisions. Thank you that you have promised in your Word that you will provide me with wisdom and knowledge as I seek after you. Thank you for the gift of the Holy Spirit empowering me to make wise decisions even when I am faced with pressures and constraints that make it seemingly impossible to be wise and knowledgeable.

An Ancient Secret to Improve
Decision-Making Skills

DARIN W. WHITE

"Make your ear attentive to wisdom, incline your heart to under-standing; For if you cry for discernment, lift your voice for under-standing; If you seek her as silver, and search for her as for hidden treasures; Then you will discern the fear of the LORD, and discover the knowledge of God. For the LORD gives wisdom; From his mouth come knowledge and understanding. He stores up sound wisdom for the upright; He is a shield to those who walk in integrity, guarding the paths of justice, and he preserves the way of his godly ones."

(Prov. 2:2–8 NAS)

A S BUSINESS professionals, we often search for that illusive degree or certification that will move us up the ladder of corporate success. We think, "If I just had an MBA from Harvard or a Ph.D. from Northwestern, then I would possess the knowledge that would launch me to true success." Striving for such accomplishments is worthy and honorable, but consid-er the quality of decision-making available to us if we endeavor to discover the knowledge of God. Wisdom that God grants allows us to see potential difficulties in business transactions be-fore they actually come to fruition. Such wisdom helps us find solutions that others have failed to consider. Steeped in God's wisdom, we have an inner confidence that allows us to overcome any obstacle and complete the task at hand. Knowledge of God grants us the ability to discern when an employee or customer is lying. Solomon had and used this ability when two women came to his court with a baby both claimed as their own (1 Kings 3:16–28). Having earnestly sought the wisdom of the

Lord, Solomon threatened to cut the child in half and give each woman part. The lying woman readily accepted his decision while the other implored him not to harm the baby, but instead give it to her rival. God granted Solomon the ability to discern the true mother and make the right decision. Like Solomon, God will grant you the ability to make the right decision when you earnestly seek his wisdom.

Lord, I pray that I will never forget to continually seek your wisdom with an earnest heart. I know that true knowledge comes only from you and that time spent mining the pages of scripture for your silver nuggets will be of infinite value to me as I walk through the world of business each day. Please grant me your wisdom so that I might make decisions that bring glory to you each and every hour of the day.

Wisdom

Ardith Baker

"For the Lord gives wisdom, and from his mouth
come knowledge and understanding."
(Prov. 2:6)

In Proverbs 2, Solomon extols the benefits and importance of wisdom. We should spend our lives seeking out wisdom, applying our hearts to understanding, calling out for insight, and crying aloud for understanding (Prov. 2:3). But from where do we get wisdom and understanding? Solomon gives us the answer: wisdom comes from God, the source of knowledge and creator of heaven and earth, and from his Word, the Bible. What are the benefits of wisdom? Why seek wisdom when we seem to have all of the information we need in our information-laden society? Information abounds from consumer surveys, marketing reports, business profiles, quarterly and weekly reports, data mining, research studies, journals, newspapers, and other media; the list goes on and on. Perhaps a better question in our information-rich age is "How can we not seek wisdom?" When we have so many choices, so much information, it is prudent to go to God first and ask for wisdom so we will "understand what is right and just and fair," choosing "every good path" (Prov. 2:9). The search for wisdom leads to knowledge, which in turn leads to discretion and discernment, both of which will be beneficial in making good business decisions.

Lord, I humbly ask for your guidance today. I recognize my human mind is limited and ask you to expand my understanding that I might increase my knowledge of you and gain wisdom. Amen.

Keep to the Paths of the Just

RICH RUDEBOCK

*"Therefore walk in the ways of the good,
and keep to the paths of the just."*
(Prov. 2:20 NRSV)

O UR DAYS are filled with many opportunities to either deviate from or stay on the "paths of the just." Throughout my career, I have lived by a personal code of conduct in which I simply ask myself, "How would I feel about explaining to my mother anything that I said or did during the day? Would I be embarrassed by my words or actions?" The reality is that while my mother is not with me every minute of the day, Jesus is. Would I be embarrassed explaining my words or actions to him? The honest answer is sometimes "yes." Fortunately, Jesus forgives me. As business professionals, we understand the value of maintaining our focus and keeping our eyes on the goal. In order to accomplish this, we spend countless hours developing mission statements and strategic plans. Jim Collins, in his book *Good to Great,* identifies eleven companies that understand the value of the "Hedgehog Concept," which is "a basic principle or concept that unifies and guides everything" they do.[2] While Jesus forgives me when I deviate from the "paths of the just," the world of business is not always so forgiving. Whether in our personal life or in business, our objective should always be to glorify God by keeping to the "Hedgehog Concept"—by keeping to the "paths of the just."

2. Jim Collins, *Good to Great* (New York: HarperCollins Publishers, Inc., 2001), 91.

Father, I pray that you will keep me aware of your presence today as you help me to walk in the ways of the good and keep to the paths of the just.

Trust and Acknowledge the Lord

Marshal H. Wright

*"Trust in the Lord with all your heart and lean not
on your own understanding; in all your ways acknowledge him,
and he will make your paths straight."*

(Prov. 3:5–6)

TRUST HAS been defined as the level of "one's confidence in and willingness to open oneself up to fair and aboveboard dealings with the other party."[3] Exchange theory of organizational development explains and predicts that this type of trust is developed within the context of relationship and experience, where trust is exchanged as a result of a track record of trustworthy interactive behavior. This is why Proverbs 3 specifically relates trusting in the Lord to the Lord directing our paths as we acknowledge him. If we take the opportunity to look for and acknowledge the Lord's involvement in every aspect of our lives (including in our business endeavors), we will discover that as we turn to him, he is faithful to guide and direct us. This interactive exchange equips us to better trust in him because he is indeed trustworthy. Try it and you will find yourself on an incredible relationship journey where the Lord continually demonstrates his immeasurable trustworthiness to you as you place greater and greater trust in him!

Lord, I want to take this moment to reflect back and thank you for continually being faithful in directing and guiding me

3. Yi-hui Huang, "OPRA: A Cross-Cultural, Multiple-Item Scale for Measuring Organization—Public Relationships," *Journal of Public Relations Research* 13, no. 1 (2001): 66, 61–90.

through this life's journey. Thank you for being a personal God, one who is always there by my side. I firmly commit to intentionally acknowledging your guiding presence in my life every day and in every circumstance. I am placing my trust in you because you are trustworthy. Thank you, Lord!

Giving Sacrificially

VICKIE SHAMP ELLIS

*"Honor the Lord with your possessions, and with the firstfruits of all
your increase; So your barns will be filled with plenty,
and your vats will overflow with new wine."*

(Prov. 3:9–10 NKJ)

DURING OUR daughter's sophomore year at Indiana
University, she called and shared that she felt led to give
her savings to her church. She explained how she'd been pray-
ing about sacrificial giving and how her church's ministry was
far-reaching. I knew she loved her church, yet never expected
her to give all the money she had been saving for a flight and
semester abroad in Germany. I couldn't imagine God calling a
poor college student to make such a sacrifice. Surely God only
required such sacrifice from the rich. After I put down the
phone, I asked my husband, "What would you say to her?" He
responded, "I'd say, I'm proud of you." Humbled, I prayed and
asked God how we could raise enough money for her flight. By
the end of September though, Nola received a scholarship for
essentially the same amount she had given her church. She told
us that God was teaching her "a big lesson about obedience." I'm
convinced the lesson was directed to her mother. Within weeks,
another scholarship was awarded, and then she was awarded the
prestigious *Herman B Wells Scholarship*—one of only three such
scholars chosen for the entire Indiana University campus. That
award trumped all her other scholarships, paid for her travel
expense and entire year abroad, her senior year back at IU, all
conferences, and more. Her barns were filled. As professionals,

we should learn a lesson from Nola. No matter how sacrificial our gift, we can't out-give God.

God, please allow me to learn more faithfulness from those godly individuals you placed in my life. Let me be a role model by celebrating your love through sacrificial giving.

Discretion

JULIE HUNTLEY

*"My son, let them not depart from your eyes—keep sound wisdom
and discretion so they will be life to your soul and grace
to your neck. Then you will walk safely in your way,
and your foot will not stumble."*

(Prov. 3:21–23 NKJV)

DEMOGRAPHIC SHIFTS have presented a challenging work environment characterized by a high degree of diversity in gender and culture. Sound wisdom and discretion are critical in this environment. Wise business people are discreet in word and action—cautious in conduct. That is, they are careful about what they say and do in the presence of others—making wise choices, being careful not to offend. When you prepare to do or say something, determine first *if this is the right thing to do*? Would this be considered an honorable thing to say or do *in the sight of everyone*? Guard your tongue. Guard your actions. Use discretion and wisdom in all your business dealings. Demonstrate courtesy and respect for the ideas, opinions, and feelings of others no matter what the gender, skin color, or ethnicity. Research confirms that this openness when dealing with others leads to more satisfying relationships with business colleagues. Remember, God shows no partiality. If we want to experience "grace to our neck"—his favor around us—neither should we be partial! As we deal wisely with others, being discreet in word and action, we can "walk safely" in this diverse work environment.

Heavenly Father, in Jesus' name, I ask that you help me to appreciate the unique differences you have created in each of us. As I endeavor to speak your heart into the lives of others, please place a guard on my lips that I may not offend, but rather minister. I commit all of my words and actions to you to be a blessing to others and to bring you glory. Thank you, Father, for directing my thoughts and causing me to succeed as I renew my mind to your Word.

Have You Given Today?

David Dyson

"Do not withhold good from those who deserve it,
when it is in your power to act."

(Prov. 3:27)

ONE CURRENT business book purports that the customer
is second. Who then is first? The employee is. Good
employees are a blessing and the product of a generous spirit.
A manager should never withhold the resources from an employee that are necessary for excellence. When the supervisor
withholds praise, he has robbed a seed (Luke 8:5–18). That
good seed, a kind word in season, will multiply in the right
environment (corporate culture) and eventually will be shared
with the customers the employee serves. When salaries are not
generous, then employees are tempted to feel undervalued and
may be forced to work a second job, diverting full attention
and allegiance from their primary employer. Companies like
QuikTrip and Chick-fil-A are noted for their dedicated and
hard-working employees. Not withholding good from their
employees, these companies emphasize personal and professional development of their staff and reap the benefits. Don't
let this day slip by without giving your employees, co-workers,
friends, or family a little praise. It will go a long way.

Father, "may the words of my mouth and the meditation of my
heart be pleasing in your sight" (Ps. 19:14). May I be both genuine
and generous in my praise of others. Help me to be like Barnabas,
an encourager. Amen.

Shine

DAVID DYSON

"But the path of the just is like the shining sun,
that shines ever brighter unto the perfect day."

(Prov. 4:18 NKJV)

ONE RULE in ethical decision-making is the "Mama Rule." This criterion states that you should not make any decision that you would not feel proud to tell in detail to your mother or to her friends. Another is the *New York Times* rule, which states that you should never do anything that you would feel uncomfortable about reading as a cover story of the next morning's edition of the *New York Times.* God's people, the just, must behave in an honorable manner in order to be sparkling examples of Christ that shine even in full daylight. Intentionally Christian universities explicitly state their missions as being "Christ centered" and often refer to "servant leadership" as an intended outcome. At my own university, Oral Roberts University, God's commissioning is well known: "[R]aise up your students to hear My voice, to go where My voice is heard small, and My healing power is not known, even to the uttermost bounds of the earth. . . ." God calls all Christian business professionals to walk in the ever-brightening light of God's favor. After all, your life may be the only witness to Christ that someone sees. Is your life shining so bright that it is noticeable not only in darkness but also at midday?

Jesus, shine in and through me. Help me be a reflection of your love and purity. Let the light of Christ be so evident in me that it becomes a light for the path of life. In Jesus' name, Amen.

The Issues of Life

Julie Huntley

*"Keep your heart with all diligence, for out of it
spring the issues of life."*

(Prov. 4:23 NKJV)

THE CONDITION of your heart—your inner man, your spirit—is critical to success in business. From your spirit flow
the issues that bring life into your work environment. Have you
ever experienced a dead situation? Think of those times when you
needed an idea for a presentation or a solution for a problem,
and there was just nothing happening in the mental arena—a
dead situation. The workplace is often plagued with similar life-
less encounters. Consider, for example, an account team trying to
come up with an idea for an advertising slogan when there is just
nothing coming. Or, consider the account team that hits the pro-
verbial brick wall when trying to develop a strategy for recovering
a customer with a competitive install base. At these times, you
will be glad you "kept your heart with all diligence" by feeding
on the Word of God. When the brain seems dead, your spirit
can bring forth issues of life into the situation. The Word of God
is full of the life of God (John 6:63). The Word deposits the life
of God into your spirit and into your situation. The Holy Spirit
will witness with your spirit, bringing you ideas, concepts, and
insights. As you speak the Word of Life over your dead situations,
you can experience the abundance of life (John 10:10), bringing
forth fruit in challenging business encounters.

*Heavenly Father, in Jesus' name, I ask that you help me to
diligently pursue the activities that feed my spirit. As I read your*

Word and spend daily time in prayer and fellowship with you, I expect your inspired ideas and your inspired opportunities in my life. I determine not to be distracted by anything that would steal my time from you. Thank you, Father, for bringing your light and life into my daily encounters as I enjoy time in your presence.

Seductive Deals

DAVID WESLEY WHITLOCK

"[T]he lips of an adulteress drip honey, and her speech is smoother than oil; but in the end she is bitter as gall, sharp as a double-edged sword. Her feet go down to death; her steps lead straight to the grave."

(Prov. 5:3–5)

G IVING ADVICE regarding immoral relationships may seem a strange backdrop for business wisdom, but the principle holds true whether discussing immorality in personal behavior or professional life. In fact, there is a rather strong parallel between avoiding sexual impurity and avoiding ungodly business practices. A seducer charms with flattering words of enticement as sweet as honey, but in the end the experience is sinful and leaves bitterness instead. So too can a business deal seem so tempting and sound so enticing that it is difficult to turn down. Business can be seductive. But no matter how tempting, if a business proposition is outside of legal, moral, and ethical bounds, it should be as off-limits as adultery and prostitution. Strong words, yet many a bitter end in a business deal was entered into by promises and smooth words dripping with honey. The best advice for dealing with such immorality: "Keep to a path far from her, do not go near the door of her house" (Prov. 5:8).

Father, keep my path far from immorality and keep me immune to the sweet seduction of those actions that promise splendor but in the end are bitter and lead to death and destruction.

Antics

DAVID DYSON

"Go to the ant, you sluggard!
Consider her ways and be wise."

(Prov. 6:6 NKJV)

THE TINY ant. Have you ever observed ants as they go about their work? They carry their own weight and then some. Have you ever noticed that there are no manager or supervisor ants? The ants work cooperatively and do not need to be told to work. They are constant workers. As a child I developed a grudge against these little creatures after having been stung by several fire ants. After that, I delighted in destroying ant hills, frequently with water. Do you know what ants do after being washed out? They build again. Adversity cannot stop the ant. Ants also store up rations before the winter. They work while it is still day, always preparing and always working. It is little wonder that God's people are instructed to consider the ways of the ant. God wants us to work unto him, heartily, and not unto man (or manager). Paul writes in Colossians, "Whatever you do, do it heartily, as to the Lord and not to men" (Col. 3:23 NKJV). We work for God—not for the company.

First, Father, we thank you for work. So many in this world envy the opportunity we have. Help us leverage this opportunity so that the blessings overflow and there is abundance to be shared. Amen.

When You Get What You Want,
Will You Want What You Get?

Sharon Johnson

"With her many persuasions she entices him; with her flattering lips she seduces him. Suddenly he follows her, as an ox goes to the slaughter, or as one in fetters to the discipline of a fool. Until an arrow pierces through his liver; as a bird hastens to the snare, so he does not know that it will cost him his life."

(Prov. 7:21–23 NAS)

SUCCESSFUL BUSINESS people are goal driven. They seek to achieve significant performance targets, to reach important milestones, and to enjoy the rewards of their efforts. They often inspire others to greater efforts through their energy and tenacity. Achievement, performance, inspiring others, and reward seeking are not wrong. Paul spoke to his own drive for accomplishing significant goals: "Brethren, I do not regard myself as having laid hold of it yet; but one thing I do: forgetting what lies behind and reaching forward to what lies ahead, I press on toward the goal for the prize of the upward call of God in Christ Jesus" (Phil. 3:13–14 NAS). Business people need to carefully examine their motives—just *why* and *for whom* are they striving after what they seek? The young and foolish man in Proverbs 7:21–23 pursued his goals with passion rather than prudence, seeking self-satisfaction rather than service, and in the end lost so much more than he gained. Perhaps he should have been *good-seeking* rather than *goal-seeking*.

Lord, lead me to seek goals that honor you and serve others. Let my life be a testimony to service rather than to self, and help me to be engaged in pursuit of eternal values rather than temporary satisfactions.

With Wisdom Comes Knowledge

Ardith Baker

"I, wisdom, dwell together with prudence;
I possess knowledge and discretion."

(Prov. 8:12)

HOW MANY knowledgeable people do you know? Perhaps you consider yourself to be an expert on a subject. Many spend their whole lives seeking knowledge, accumulating vast amounts of information in the belief that it will elevate them above others in their profession or give them a competitive edge in business. Perhaps we are all guilty of wanting to know more so that we can get ahead and make a name for ourselves. But what good is knowledge if you do not have the wisdom to use it appropriately? Certainly, knowledge does not imply wisdom. When Solomon described wisdom, he said that it possesses "knowledge and discretion." With wisdom comes knowledge and discretion. In other words, when we ask for wisdom from God, he provides us not only with the knowledge that we need but also the discretion to use it appropriately. Knowledge is good and important. There is nothing wrong with wanting to get ahead in business or make a name for ourselves. However, if we keep our focus on God and start each day by asking God for wisdom, he will provide us with the means to acquire knowledge that we need and the discretion to use it wisely with successful results. Rely on God to provide you with all your needs; trust in him to give you wisdom to handle any situation so that you will not fail.

Father, help me to maintain my focus on you each day. I pray for wisdom and thank you for providing for all my needs, including my need to learn and improve my knowledge base in this competitive world.

Where You Live and Where You Walk

Phillip V. Lewis

"I am Lady Wisdom, and I live next to Sanity; Knowledge and Discretion live just down the street. . . You can find me on Righteous Road—that's where I walk—at the intersection of Justice Avenue."

(Prov. 8:12, 20 MSG)

I HEARD of a commencement speaker who proclaimed, "In five years, one-half of everything you've learned will be obsolete. I wish I could tell you which half." It reminded me of a book by Tony Campolo: *Everything You've Heard Is Wrong*. If such warnings are correct, we should seriously ponder these questions:

What kind of person should I be? Character is the result of every decision you make. Over time, you become who you are. Wisdom says you should be living in sanity, knowledge, discretion, righteousness, and justice.

What kind of work should I do? We are to be engaged in honest labor that glorifies God. Every year some lose jobs because they refuse to lie and cheat. Is that price worth paying? Absolutely, if it means you continue to walk at the intersection of "Justice Avenue" and "Righteous Road."

What will my legacy be? What kind of difference do I make in people's lives? I attended the funeral of a colleague who had made the purpose of his life a commitment to leave behind something of significance. He succeeded. We ought to consider what will be our own legacy.

If everything you've learned will be out of date in two or three years, and if everything you've heard is wrong, you ought to be doing all you can to follow in the footsteps of "Lady Wisdom." Like her, you must recognize the necessity of understanding who you are, what you will do, and what you will leave behind.

Father, help me in my commitment to live next to sanity, down the street from knowledge and discretion, and may I be found at the intersection of Righteous Road and Justice Avenue. Glorify your son as I live my life in that neighborhood.

Correction, Instruction, and Teaching

Marshal H. Wright

*"[R]ebuke a wise man and he will love you. Instruct a wise man
and he will be wiser still; teach a righteous man
and he will add to his learning."*

(Prov. 9:8b–9)

IN TODAY's rapidly changing and highly competitive business
environments, many leaders are rallying their organizations
around a culture of *problem solving*. In this context, one of the
most valued forms of capital is "information and knowledge"
and a preferred organizational environment is that of a "learning organization."[4] Richard Daft identifies a "learning organization" as one that "promotes communication and collaboration"
through an organizational development system that is "based
on equality, open information, little hierarchy, and a culture
that encourages adaptability and participation, enabling ideas
to bubble up from anywhere that can help the organization
seize opportunities and handle crises."[5] When this occurs, the
individual is empowered, and the organization normally excels.
In these types of organizations, information, knowledge, and
control of tasks are all produced primarily through employee
collaboration and initiative rather than being a product of su-
pervisory or executive control and direction. However, in order
for this type of organizational structure to exist and be effective, the members of the organization must welcome correction,
instruction, and teaching from others and not just from those

4. Richard L. Daft, *Organization Theory and Design*, 7th ed. (Cincinnati: South-Western College Publishing, 2001), 25.

5. Ibid.

in authoritative positions. In other words, Proverbs 9:8b–9 succinctly describes model workers in such organizations.

Lord, I pray that you, through the power of the Holy Spirit, will give me a humble heart and spirit. I pray that you will empower me to hear from those around me and that I will better welcome correction, instruction, and teaching so that I can become a better functioning and contributing member of the body of Christ.

Tsunami Relief

CHRIS PUTMAN

"I wisdom, will make the hours of your day more profitable."
(Prov. 9:11 TLB)

As my husband and I unloaded four moving vans full of furniture into our newly built home, I panned the ceiling high stacks of boxes and panicked at my undertaking. The walls were stark, and the new house had no personality. I had sixty days before the fall semester to settle, make curtains and install blinds for fourteen windows, wallpaper eight rooms, paint furniture, stencil archways, decorate, and landscape, in addition to teaching four summer classes and reading several new textbooks. Whenever I looked at the big picture of all I had to do, I panicked. I felt I was standing at the foot of a mammoth, swelling tidal wave. Trying to swallow a tsunami whole was a monumental, overwhelming task. One day while complaining to God about my workload, he spoke. As usual with me, he said much with only a few words: "Get your spoon out." Mulling it over, I finally got it. Don't look at the big picture; instead eat the elephant one bite at a time. One single task is never overwhelming, so I focused on only what was directly in front of me. With that job done, I focused on the next. Amazed, by day 58, I had swallowed my tsunami. Many times since, I've shared my experience of swallowing a tsunami with my panicky, overwhelmed students and co-workers. Every so often, as I pass a former student in the busy academic hallways, I hear one yell, "Hey, professor, I've got my spoon out."

Lord, help us to prioritize what you would have us to tackle first on our "To Do" lists. Help us to not be intimidated by the size of the list, but instead to focus on what you put directly before us. Give us the wisdom and ability to conquer that one task so that we can move on to the next.

Remember Me

Ardith Baker

*"The memory of the righteous will be a blessing,
but the name of the wicked will rot."*

(Prov. 10:7)

How will you be remembered? In this day and age, job changes (whether voluntary or involuntary) are frequent. So, how will you be remembered by those you leave in your previous job? Will they talk about you with fondness, remembering all the contributions that you made to the company? Will they value your friendship? Would they want you to come back? Or, will relief and gladness at your leaving be the focus of their conversations? Wouldn't you rather be remembered as a blessing than as a curse? If so, then here is what you need to do:

- First and foremost, set your sights not on personal gain, but on God—live a righteous and holy life at work as well as at home so that your actions will be a reflection of the loving God that you serve.

- Treat everyone with whom you come into contact with respect and dignity, valuing their contribution (no matter how small) to the company.

- Take advantage of every opportunity that comes your way so that you will increase your knowledge and skills and ultimately your worth to the company.

- Work diligently for the benefit of your company, even up to your very last day of employment with them.

Then, you will gain respect and admiration from those with whom you work and your memory will be a blessing.

Lord, please give me a servant's heart today as I walk in your will. Allow me to serve you by serving your children—my co-workers and bosses. Allow them to see your glory through me so that they may be drawn closer to you.

And Then Some

Chris Putman

*"People with integrity have firm footing,
but those who follow crooked paths will slip and fall."*
(Prov. 10:9 NLT)

I DON'T work for my boss. I remind myself daily that I work for the Lord, realizing that the Lord sees what my boss doesn't. When I work for the Lord, I simply allow excellence and integrity to rule every task I undertake. Instead of arriving at the office on time, I arrive early. Instead of racing from the workplace at quitting time, I often linger to accomplish a few more tasks. I don't *meet* my deadlines; instead, I finish them early. I often take projects home to work on in a quiet, uninterrupted atmosphere where my best ideas have a propensity to hatch. When I receive a voicemail, I am prompt to return the call; when I receive an e-mail, I am timely in my response. Business casual dress is allowed, but I show up every day dressed as if I were going for an interview. Why? Because I work for the Lord. I know I can easily skirt by with an 80 percent effort, but I *want* to do my very best work for the Lord; I *want* to go that extra mile. Whatever is expected, I want to deliver just a bit more. If I am truly working for Jesus, I want to use integrity as the ruler by which I measure my actions. So, when you work for the Lord, settle for nothing less than excellence. Desire to do a good job—and then some.

Lord, let excellence shine in my life—not just to draw attention to myself or for a raise or promotion—but to let others see you in me. Help me to be upright in all I do . . . and then some.

Be Wise in the Long Run

Susan Lynch

*"When words are many, sin is not absent,
but he who holds his tongue is wise."*
(Prov. 10:19)

IT IS just plain hard to withhold angry words against someone who is mean and ugly to us. Who do they think they are to treat us in such a manner? Too often our human nature is to lash back at anyone and everyone who angers or criticizes us. They hurt us, so we feel the need to hurt them back. In so doing, we hope to feel better about ourselves. We want to get even; we want revenge. But when we do strike back, do we really feel better about ourselves? Does our retaliatory outburst really even the score? Worse yet, after lashing out at the offender, do we feel any better about our relationship with that person or our relationship with God? Has the situation been improved? Have we really won? Is our anger really gone, or has it continued to gnaw at us, raising our blood pressure, heart rate, and stress level? What other options do we have in responding to an angry person? Turn the other cheek? Be kind? Surely you jest. Being kind and turning the other cheek is certainly not the easy way out, nor is it guaranteed to make us feel better. Or would it? Can holding our tongue really be the best way to handle a verbally abusive individual? In the short run, our thought may be "no," but Proverbs reminds us, "he who holds his tongue is wise." And being wise, we know, is always better in the long run.

Help me Father to hold my tongue, to control my thoughts, actions, and especially my words as I deal with colleagues and customers.

38

Laziness

*"As vinegar to the teeth and smoke to the eyes,
so is a lazy man to those who send him."*
(Prov. 10:26 NKJV)

THE EMPLOYER-EMPLOYEE relationship is important to God. He wants us to understand those characteristics that will cause us to prosper in our business relationships. In this way, he can empower us to succeed (Deut. 8:18). Here we are told of one work habit that will prevent success in the workplace—laziness. Consider the harmful effects of laziness. Have you ever been sitting around a campfire when the wind shifts and blows smoke into your eyes? Not only does it cloud your vision, but it also brings pain and discomfort by causing your eyes to sting. The employer who works with a lazy employee experiences a clouded vision with regard to the true qualities of the individual—unable to see clearly the good work habits that may be displayed. The employer further experiences the pain of unmet expectations and lack of productivity. Think for moment about having a mouth full of vinegar. The taste of vinegar meets with a strong aversion because of intolerance for its acidic bitterness. It literally causes you to grit your teeth; it sets your teeth on edge. Like a mouth full of vinegar, an employer reacts strongly and has little tolerance for a lazy employee. Don't be lazy! The effects are harmful to your business career. The zealous and eager employee who demonstrates a passion for his or her work should be embraced and rewarded.

Heavenly Father, in Jesus' name, I ask that you help me to do what is right for my employer. Even as I do all of my work unto you, help me to take initiative and diligently accomplish my employer's goals. I desire to respect and honor my employer as I honor and respect you. Thank you, Father, for empowering me to do your perfect will in the workplace.

Honest Scales

David Wesley Whitlock

"The LORD abhors dishonest scales,
but accurate weights are his delight."
(Prov. 11:1)

A N OLD Norman Rockwell painting—*Tipping the Scales*—
graced the cover of the *Saturday Evening Post* on October 3,
1936, and shows an older woman and a grocer staring up at the
scale as they weighed the purchase. With innocent stares, each
of them was attempting to cheat the other, the old woman with
her finger on the bottom of the scale lifting up, the grocer with
his finger atop the scale pressing down. Though meant to be a
humorous depiction of commerce, dealing fairly in business is, in
fact, a serious matter with God. His Word commands that business be transacted in a completely honest fashion. God hates—he
abhors—dishonest scales. Another proverb states, "Honest scales
and balances are from the LORD; all the weights in the bag are
of his making" (Prov. 16:11). And in Leviticus, God commands,
"Use honest scales and honest weights, an honest ephah and an
honest hin. I am the LORD your God, who brought you out
of Egypt" (Lev. 19:36). Honest scales—fair and equitable business—is a matter of scriptural integrity. For the Christian business
professional, it's not just good business practice, it's a critical matter of obedience. Accurate weights are his delight.

Help me, Father, to be fair and equitable in all of my business
transactions. Let no hint of dishonesty in my business be found. Take
delight in my obedience to your Word and my commitment to use
honest scales and accurate weights. Forgive me where I have failed
and direct me to make it right.

Humility

Ardith Baker

*"When pride comes, then comes disgrace,
but with humility comes wisdom."*
(Prov. 11:2)

THERE THEY are, bragging again about everything that they've done. They're getting all the credit, and I did all the work! Why doesn't anyone notice the good job that I'm doing? Why don't I get the attention that I deserve? Maybe I should just speak out and brag on myself, just a little. But wait, something nags at me. What are my motives? Who am I trying to promote, myself or my company? After all, who am I here to serve? If you can answer these questions honestly, and if you truly desire to serve God in your workplace, then you will realize that praise from man is not what you're seeking or what you need. When we brag about our experiences and accomplishments, pride tends to take over, and all of a sudden we seem to be pushing people away with our puffed-up self image instead of drawing them to us and our achievements. Remain humble and do your job earnestly and patiently, maintaining God as your focus. Be proud, not prideful, of the gifts and talents that God has given you, and use them to serve God in your workplace. In this way, your co-workers, supervisors, and managers will be drawn to you and your ability to handle situations or tasks quietly, efficiently, and with wisdom. Your good works will not go unnoticed by your company or most importantly, by God. After all, we ultimately serve—work for—God.

Lord, thank you for the position you have placed me in. Please grow the vision in my heart to be a humble instrument you can use. Please direct my mind, words, and actions to be used wisely in my workplace. Amen.

The Influence of a Leader

Marshal H. Wright

*"Through the blessing of the upright a city is exalted,
but by the mouth of the wicked, it is destroyed."*
(Prov. 11:11)

THROUGH HIS research on organizational culture and leadership, Edgar Schein identified several "primary embedding mechanisms" by which leaders teach and influence their organizational membership to subscribe to a certain culture or to follow a particular course of action. Schein identifies some of these embedding mechanisms:

- "What leaders pay attention to, measure, and control on a regular basis"

- "How leaders react to critical incidents and organizational crises"

- "Observed criteria by which leaders allocate scarce resources"

- "Deliberate role modeling, teaching, and coaching"

- "Observed criteria by which leaders allocate rewards and status" and

- "Observed criteria by which leaders recruit, select, promote, retire, and excommunicate organizational members"[6]

6. Edgar H. Schein, *Organizational Culture and Leadership*, 2nd ed. (San Francisco: Jossey-Bass Publishers, 1992), 231.

As Christian business leaders, we have the ability to exalt or destroy our organizations by the influence we exert over our colleagues and the organizational culture. The more we apply Schein's embedding mechanisms to demonstrate the value of righteousness and to inculcate cultures of *uprightness*, the greater the organizations we work within will be exalted! Pray for guidance on how you can be a blessing to your organization by better influencing those around you.

Lord, I pray that your Holy Spirit will guide and direct my paths as I interact with those around me. I pray that I will be a blessing to all I come into contact with and that I will recognize opportunities to represent you by influencing others toward righteousness and upright behavior.

Hold Your Tongue

ARDITH BAKER

*"A man who lacks judgment derides his neighbor,
but a man of understanding holds his tongue."*
(Prov. 11:12)

IT WAS a few minutes before the meeting would start, and we were all entering the room. Seated at the table with me was a co-worker who had no problem criticizing his fellow workers. He had the ability to make his cruel remarks seem like a joke, laughing off each one after he said them. At this meeting, he was suddenly on the attack, taking pointed jabs at a fellow worker as she came in and sat down. They were clearly unfair remarks said out of jealousy and pride. My co-worker was visibly wounded, but she said nothing as she sat down. Obviously, the tone for the meeting was set. I was upset and desperately wanted to come to her defense. But instead, I said nothing. In fact, no one said anything; we just started the meeting. Should I have jumped to her aid? On the one hand, I was afraid that if I did, I would be his next victim. On the other hand, it wasn't my battle. Should she have defended herself against this verbal attack? I don't know, but Proverbs clearly states that a person of understanding holds his or her tongue. You must consider each situation and all possible outcomes before deciding for yourself. Check your spirit for guidance and discretion. Though there are indeed times when we should come to the aid or defense of another, often, the best thing to do is to just hold your tongue.

Father, help me to know when I should speak up or when I should stay quiet. When the time is right to speak, give me the appropriate words to say and the boldness to say them. When it is time for me to stay quiet, give me peace of mind and the assurance that I am doing the right thing. Amen.

Secrets

David Dyson

"A talebearer reveals secrets,
But he who is of a faithful spirit conceals the matter."
(Prov. 11:13 NKJV)

Have you ever been tempted to reveal some truth about your rival or enemy? Perhaps you have information that would make you look so much better if others only knew. This proverb reveals the gracious spirit of God that can be ours: "A faithful spirit conceals the matter." What would God do? God in his grace asks us to acknowledge our sin and to confess him. He does not ask us to shout the sin from housetops. His grace allows our mistakes to be forgiven, and he asks that we focus on him, not the sin. In like manner one should adopt the character of God and extend that grace to others. The flesh suggests we expose our competitors and tell all their faults. God's plan is different. In Romans 12:20 the believer is instructed to take care of his enemies. By so doing one will heap hot coals of fire on the enemy's head. Choose to be godly and gracious.

Father, you have said in your Word that life and death are in the tongue (Prov. 18:21). Help us to choose life and speak only those words that edify. Teach us to be like you, merciful and slow to anger. Help us hold our tongue if the words are less than pure, and help us be courageous when we need to speak words of praise. Amen

Compensation

JOSEPH J. BUCCI

"The wicked earns deceptive wages,
but he who sows righteousness gets a true reward."
(Prov. 11:18 NAS)

ONE OF the great debates among workers in a business is whether or not they are compensated fairly for their work. Generally the criticisms come about due to comparisons workers make with the wages and perks received by others. A good human resources practice is to establish a pay policy based on the organization's strategic objectives and in ways that motivate workers towards greater performance.[7] One of the most critical parts of this process is communication.[8] People seem to be more suspect of others' compensation when they are unaware of the process or are not given input into plan design. Ultimately we know that as Christians our happiness in not derived from this world's rewards alone, but from the treasures we store in heaven (Matt. 6:20–21). This "not yet" type of reward system may be initially frustrating, but here in the proverb, Solomon tells us that there is also an immediate benefit to being other-worldly-minded. Sowing hard work or giving of our time and efforts to an earthly employer may give us some kind of return for our efforts, but it will never fully satisfy us. Our reward for

---

7. This and many other thoughts related to developing a strategic compensation system can be found in George T. Milkovich and Jerry Newman, *Compensation* (New York: McGraw-Hill/Irwin, 2005).

8. Raymond Andrew Noe, et al., *Fundamentals of Human Resource Management*, 2nd ed. (New York: McGraw-Hill/Irwin, 2007).

sowing goodness and right actions is a sure one that can never be taken away by loss of status, downsizing, transfer, deferred promotion, or lack of recognition. We know he who is watching will surely be faithful to keep his commitments. Proverbs 10:16, 22:4, 25:22 give us more of this good advice.

We know that you are faithful in forgiveness and in carrying out your perfect plan in and through our lives. We trust your Word when you say you will be faithful to reward our righteous actions on your behalf, whether or not our employer fully appreciates our value. We move with confidence, knowing that you will supply all our needs according to your riches in glory in Christ Jesus.

Generosity

Timothy DeClue

"A generous man will prosper;
he who refreshes others will himself be refreshed."

(Prov. 11:25)

A NEW friend once spent an entire Saturday with me working on an old (even then) 1971 Ford pickup. Neither of us knew very much about what we were doing, but we both enjoyed each other's company and twenty years later he and I still remember that day and chuckle about it. I'm sure he had other things to do, but instead he chose to help me and in doing so turned a frustrating task into a lifelong memory. What a generous gift of his time and friendship he gave that day! How are you generous? We usually think about generosity only in terms of finances, but giving money is perhaps the least effective way to be generous. Think about the people who have had a significant impact on your life. Was their memorable generosity in the form of cash? Likely not. Instead their generosity was related to time, love, expertise, friendship, advice, and hospitality—almost anything except money! God encourages generosity in us because he is generous. What will you be generous with today?

Make me a generous person who refreshes others, Lord. And I will refresh myself in you.

Discipline and Correction

Walter MacMillan

*"Whoever loves discipline loves knowledge, but he
who hates correction is stupid. A good man obtains favor
from the Lord, but the Lord condemns a crafty man."*

(Prov. 12:1–2)

THIS PROVERB addresses one of the major and most talked
about problems we face in business today: the acquisition
and retention of knowledge. All organizations are keenly aware
of the necessity to acquire and retain knowledge. Organizational
success depends on gaining knowledge and the use and retention
of it. People who constantly seek new knowledge are the ones
who tend to be successful—we should never stop learning. In
previous generations, a person could graduate from a university
and have a career without further formal education. But in our
society, we can never stop learning. If we do, others will pass us
by. We must also learn to love correction—it will be the building
block to our success. Some business people have never acquired
the skill to accept correction in a positive way. When we accept
it, we will succeed, for the Lord favors a good person who loves
discipline and knowledge. We will encounter crafty people who
will enjoy short term success; however, in the long run justice
will prevail. We have seen many leaders of business fall in recent
years, proving that dishonesty brings only short-term success.
We sometimes wonder when the Lord is going to deal with the
dishonest person in our lives, but we must simply trust in the
Lord and wait for his timing. No bad deed goes uncorrected. No

one who loves discipline and knowledge and trusts in God ever goes unnoticed.

Father, provide me with opportunities to learn and to acquire the knowledge that I need for my job. At the same time, help me to accept your correction and discipline as a tool for personal growth and development. Bless all my efforts as I strive to serve you. Amen.

Hard Work

David Wesley Whitlock

"Work hard and become a leader;
be lazy and never succeed."

(Prov. 12:24 TLB)

THOUGH IT'S hard to believe in today's society, those very words hung in the public school gymnasium on the night I graduated from high school. Though it carried no citation, this proverb was our class motto and the words stuck. I thought of them often during college, early in my career, and later as a husband and parent. The words reinforced one of the principles my family taught me—work hard and avoid laziness. The work ethic was emphasized in my family. To do a job well is its own reward. The New Testament urges us, "And whatever you do, do it heartily, as to the Lord and not to men, knowing that from the Lord you will receive the reward of the inheritance; for you serve the Lord Christ" (Col. 3:23–24 NKJV). Many people seem only to be motivated to make a real effort if the boss happens to be watching. Yet, it isn't supposed to be this way for a person who professes faith in Christ. Instead, the Christian in the workplace ought to be the one counted on to be on time, to put in a fair day's labor, and to work hard as if working directly for Jesus. Jesus taught his followers that to be the greatest, they would have to become the least, to humble themselves as a servant—just like he did. If you desire greatness and leadership responsibilities, be humble and serve others. Laziness is abhorrent to the genuine Christian.

Prepare me today to work hard. Rebuke laziness in me, Father, and help me to work as unto the Lord. Amen.

Heeding Instruction

Walter MacMillan

"A wise son heeds his father's instruction, but a mocker does not listen to rebuke. From the fruit of his lips a man enjoys good things, but the unfaithful have a craving for violence. He who guards his lips guards his life, but he who speaks rashly will come to ruin."

(Prov. 13:1–3)

THIS PROVERB tells us directly the importance of listening to our peers and superiors. It reminds us that we have much to learn and the importance of listening to the advice of others. We are reminded that we are responsible for the things that we say, and those who spread rumors or untruths are destined to failure. One of the most important keys to success is learning to control our tongues. Only a limited number of people ever learn to truly control their tongues. We see it everyday in the business world. The "grapevine" is one of the most important means of communication in most organizations; however, it also carries much misinformation and damaging information. People who do not control their tongues usually end up in trouble. This proverb teaches us to listen and take advice; it teaches us to use our tongues wisely—to be careful what we say. Listen, learn, and speak with caution.

Lord, help me to be quiet and to listen with a discerning heart. Provide for me mentors who will offer godly advice and direction. Thank you for instilling in me a spirit of peace as I strive to control my thoughts and actions. Amen.

Building Walls

ARDITH BAKER

*"The wise woman builds her house, but with her own hands
the foolish one tears hers down."*

(Prov. 14:1)

MAN OR woman, we all build our "houses" around us.
Our "house" consists of our reputation, built brick by
brick, layer by layer, with our words and deeds. Each act that we
perform, each word that we speak, either lays a brick down or
takes one off. When we do a good work, our reputation is built
up and we lay a brick down. When we impatiently or foolishly
act or speak, we damage our reputation and rip a brick off the
walls. No one is perfect, and each situation that we encounter
invokes a different response in us. However, the question is this:
do we rip off more bricks than we lay down? Take a moment to
examine your reputation. How have you built your house? Do
your co-workers and employers see you as a valuable resource
and patient mentor, or as someone to be avoided, not worthy
of trust or confidence? Reputations, like walls, can be rebuilt.
It may take time and hard work, but it can be done. Start first
with the foundation. A good solid footing on which to build
your walls is imperative. The best foundation is God's written
Word—the Bible. Let the scriptures guide your life at home and
at work, and you will find that it will become easier to do good
works and to say the right things. Built on such an excellent
foundation, the walls to your house will be strong and will en-
dure the tests of time.

Thank you for giving your Son, Jesus Christ, as the perfect example of how we should live our lives. Please give me the strength and wisdom to make the right choices that will build up my house and not tear it down.

Quick, Hide Me!

ARDITH BAKER

"He who despises his neighbor sins,
but blessed is he who is kind to the needy."
(Prov. 14:21)

OH NO, here she comes again! Where can I hide in my cubicle? I know what she wants; she asks me the same computer questions over and over. I'll explain it one more time, and she still won't get it. Maybe I should suggest that she go to some classes and get some training, or maybe I should just tell her that I'm too busy to help and she's just on her own. Maybe I should complain to my boss. After all, she's taking up my precious time, and I can't get my own work done. But, I know why she comes to me. Because I will answer her questions respectfully and patiently, trying to teach her instead of just telling her what to do. I know that one of these days she *will* get it. It's frustrating, but I've been in her shoes before and needed someone to help me. Most likely I will be in her shoes again, and I hope that someone will treat me as kindly as I have tried to treat her. I also know that God will bless me for being patient and kind to those in need, especially those with whom I work. It's easy to be abrupt and brush people off, but God specifically tells us to be kind to our co-workers in need so that we may reflect his loving kindness and be his light in our workplace.

God, I give my time to you today. As your ambassador to those in need, I pray for patience and understanding so that I will best be able to serve you when a need arises throughout my day. Amen

Big Talkers

"In all labor there is profit,
but idle chatter leads only to poverty."
(Prov. 14:23 NKJV)

EVERY PLACE of work has them, it seems. Big talkers, always chattering about big plans and past glories, they live in the hope of winning the lottery, striking it rich, or inheriting some distant relative's fortune. They dream of striking it rich so they can live lives of leisure. Yet idle talk leads to poverty—not just in material blessings, but also poverty of character. God never intended work as a punishment, and contrary to the view that work was a result of the fall of man, it should be recognized that work was ordained of God prior to sin and the fall. Placing Adam in the Garden, God instructed him to tend the Garden. His sin and the fall simply perverted work in a way that made it difficult—amidst thistles and thorns and by the sweat of the brow. Work is honorable, good, and God-ordained. In Lev. 23:22, the Hebrews were instructed to leave missed or dropped grain during a harvest; they were also instructed not to harvest the corners of their fields. This was in order to allow the needy and poor an opportunity to glean. It was important that those without were given the opportunity to work. Why? Because work is good and honorable, and in all labor there is profit. But big talkers are led to poverty, either materially or worse—the poverty of character.

Forgive me for attempting to replace honorable labor with idle talk. Instill in me the God-ordained desire to work and earn what is right and fair and to remove the want of ill-gotten gain. Keep me from confusing big plans and idle chatter with honorable labor.

You Were Never in Control

BOB KLOSTERMEYER

*"The eyes of the LORD are in every place,
keeping watch on the evil and the good."*
(Prov. 15:3 NKJV)

THERE ARE times when the events of this world seem to be out of control. Turbulent times we experience can produce a sense of hopelessness. As a much younger man who had not yet experienced salvation, I tried to make sense of my slice of the world by attempting to manipulate my environment and the people around me. I buffered the events of the outside world by believing that if I could control my finite universe, all would be well. But the reality was that I never really could control my corner of the universe. You can refuse to acknowledge God's sovereignty and pretend to be master of your kingdom for only so long. During those years, I remember reading about a German couple, who—after landing in Florida for a vacation—made a wrong turn in their rental car when leaving the Miami airport. They ended up lost in a neighborhood that swiftly and brutally ended their vacation and their lives. I recall the despair I felt when I read about their senseless murders; the news reports crushed my own sense of control. Not until I came into a full-time relationship with Jesus Christ was I able to reconcile the horror of that event. In business as in life, I was never in control at all. Thankfully, God is.

God, you are in control and see everything. When the weeds of this world appear to be overtaking the beauty, I trust that you, as the Master Gardener, are seeing it all and are in control.

What Are You Hungry For?

David B. Whitlock

"A wise person is hungry for truth,
while the fool feeds on trash."

(Prov. 15:14 NLT)

WHAT WE put into our minds is every bit as important as what we put into our bodies. Just as our diet affects our physical health, so our mental diet affects our mental health. The movies we watch, the books we read—including all of those business best-sellers—and the pictures we gaze on all affect our mind. Our little miniature Schnauzer, Casey, has neither discernment nor discipline. We have to keep a close watch on her; it's dangerous to let her roam free. That's because she will eat anything that looks or smells like it might be good. One time she ate something that almost cost our little dog her life. It resulted in severe pancreatitis. We now have to watch her diet so that her stomach will not be upset. We have to discipline Casey and exercise discernment for her because she is, after all, just a dog. She would just as soon run to the trash down the street than eat the healthy food we have for her at home. Unlike little Casey, we can change the way we think and therefore change our mental appetite. The more disciplined we become in what we put into our minds, the more we acquire a hunger and thirst for the things of God rather than the trash the world offers. And that's a mark of a truly wise person.

Lord, give me a hunger and thirst for righteousness. Strengthen my resolve to stay pure and holy for you.

How Much Is Enough?

DAVID WESLEY WHITLOCK

*"Better a little with the fear of the LORD
than great wealth with turmoil."*
(Prov. 15:16)

How much is enough? It's a question worth pondering. What will it take for you to be satisfied? The American culture, sadly even in the Church, is such that we are driven to consume, driven to acquire. We want newer, better, improved. Our appetites seem insatiable, yet with possessions and wealth come stress and turmoil. Soon, we serve our possessions, being consumed and devoted to the care and protection of our stuff. This is not the way it is supposed to be with Christians. We are to be satisfied with what God has entrusted us, living in awe of the Lord Jehovah. Christ asked, "What good is it for a man to gain the whole world, and yet lose or forfeit his very self?" (Luke 9:25). In business, we often seek more for the sake of having more. Our motivation is often selfish, and as a result we are never satisfied. To have the whole world at our disposal, to completely corner the market, to be named the wealthiest person in our field sounds wonderful on the one hand. But the turmoil that accompanies such wealth pales in comparison to the one who—though she has little—has a relationship with the Lord. How much is enough?

Thank you, Father, for my relationship with you through your Son, Jesus. You are worth far more than any worldly wealth, and I ask you to help me be content, knowing that my relationship with you makes me rich.

An Apt Reply

GIL TROUT

*"A man finds joy in giving an apt reply—and how good
is a timely word!"*

(Prov. 15:23)

WE CAN all relate to receiving a phone call or note from a friend or co-worker that seemed to be just what we needed at exactly the right time. Yet, the beginning of this verse is not about receiving a timely word; it is about the joy in giving an apt reply. As we think outside ourselves, God enables us to see others' needs. He prompts us to action, nudges our hearts, and equips us with just the right message. There is amazing joy that comes in being used by God to encourage others. Fitting and suitable replies are prompted by God and can be delivered in a variety of ways: brief notes or scripture verses, a few lyrics to a song, a handwritten note, or a poem. Last Christmas I felt compelled to write a friend a note with a short poem God impressed me to compose:

> You are calling us to obedience,
> You are calling us to truth,
> You are calling us to mercy,
> You are calling us to you.

The blessing in sending this to my friend was two-fold: his receiving this timely word of encouragement and the joy I experienced in using the creative gifts and opportunity God has given me to glorify him.

Father, help us to be sensitive to the needs of others. Thank you for allowing us to be a part of your plan. May our words be pleasing to you and encouraging to those around us.

Back to Camp

VICKIE SHAMP ELLIS

*"A man has joy by the answer of his mouth,
and a word spoken in due season, how good it is."*

(Prov. 15:23 NKJ)

OFTEN, WE face trials at work or home, and at a point of despair, we hope beyond hope for some bit of wisdom or direction. As the youngest in the Shamp household, I had a rip-roaring childhood. Each summer, I resurfaced Lake Texoma with my skis; in the winter, Christmas came with turkey and presents. My siblings sold cases of fireworks and with my best friend, Tammy, I sold Girl Scout cookies. Just before my thirteenth birthday, my childhood unraveled when my big brother, Craig, died of complications sustained in a car wreck. I believed then that deep joy would never return. My family's loss transformed the "kick-the-can" life I'd known into an agonizing game of survival. I learned at my brother's hospital bed, though, that when given the chance to embrace cheerfulness, fun, and enthusiasm, I should. On my last visit with him, Craig said, "Oh Vickie, you should be at Girl Scout Camp." Those words were a kind of *wink* from my big brother—a message I've grown to appreciate more each day. He wanted me to live life to the fullest. I believe Craig's words, spoken in due season, were a gift from God. Though Craig moved on to heaven, I should continue gusto-living and "get back to camp." No matter what trial or tragedy we face in life, at home, or at work, we are called to overcome and get back to camp. In due season, may our words encourage others as Craig's words encouraged me.

God, as I share today with family, friends, and colleagues, please help me be a discerning vessel for your wisdom. Help me work with gusto, relax with gusto, and passionately embrace the delight and laughter that comes from being your child.

Commitment

ARDITH BAKER

*"Commit to the Lord whatever you do
and your plans will succeed."*

(Prov. 16:3)

WHERE CAN we go wrong if we just follow this simple piece of advice? God always has our best interests in mind, and this transfers to our business dealings as well. Do you want your company to succeed? Whether self-employed or working for someone else, we all desire to be successful. Here is a simple recipe for success: Simply commit in your heart to God your life, relationships, finances, and business, and he will guide and direct your thoughts, actions, and steps so that you will succeed! But commitment to God always involves more than just *lip service*. Not only should we purpose in our hearts to commit to God all we do on a daily basis, but we should then act on it by taking advantage of the opportunities God gives us, being obedient to serve him. In this way, God will honor our commitment, and we will be truly blessed in all aspects of our lives. After all, isn't this the true definition of success?

Make your plans my plans, God. I commit my life, relationships, finances, and profession to you. Direct my thoughts, actions, and steps. Amen.

Just Weights

TIM REDMER

"A just weight and balance are the Lord's:
all the weights of the bag are his work."

(Prov. 16:11 KJV)

FOUNDATIONAL TO accounting is the accounting equation, which indicates that assets equal liabilities plus equity. There is a balance between the resources belonging to a business entity (assets) and the sources of those resources (liabilities and equity). The balance sheet is based on the accounting equation. Accounting is based on a "just weights" philosophy. Items of worth and the resources of a company are given a monetary value, "weights," based on objective criteria at the time of acquisition, exchange, or disposal. This verse also teaches that just weights and an appropriate balance are God-ordained; "all the weights of the bag are his work." He recognized the importance of an absolute measurement and consistent standard for comparison. Reasonable and honorable men and women have come to rely and depend on this concept for their business dealings and are willing to abide by this principle. From an ethical perspective, there have to be absolutes in order to provide guidelines for appropriate actions. When we begin to interpret or modify what God identified as absolute, we fall into sin and deception. Such actions of accounting impropriety, like the case of Enron, are well-documented; the consequences can be catastrophic. God established these just weights and balances to promote order and integrity. We would be wise to follow God's provision and honor his standards.

Thank you for the order and absolute standards you have set for us. I pray that I can comply with these just weights and balances and these actions will be a reflection of my integrity. I ask for your leading and guidance and that I have the courage to remain true to your Word and principles in all that I do.

Choosing the Right Path

Ardith Baker

*"There is a way that seems right to a man,
but in the end it leads to death."*

(Prov. 16:25)

How often have we looked back on our life and realized that the path we chose was the wrong one? The way that seemed so right at the time turned out to be so wrong, resulting in emotional, spiritual, and perhaps, physical suffering. Why is it hard to make good decisions? Business decisions are often governed by worldly laws, public viewpoints, and current trends rather than by our personal relationship with God. As a result, we end up focusing solely on financial profit and professional gain, leaving God "in the dust." Although this way might seem right to man, we must recognize that we are easily deceived and influenced by our sinful nature and desires. Think of all the lives and businesses that have been destroyed because company leaders have followed this selfish path. How do you keep from following this path and make good business decisions on a daily or even hourly basis? By putting God first in your life! We need God as our conscience, guide, teacher, father, and friend. Share all your concerns with the Lord throughout the day and ask him to help you make the right decisions. God will not let you down. Turning to God first will allow you to keep all those laws, public viewpoints, and current trends in perspective; and this will allow you to utilize them as the business tools that they are. In this way, God will show you the right path to follow and bless you personally and professionally.

Your way is best, God. Even when I don't understand, lead me. I want to be obedient. Forgive me for pursuing my own way. Show me your path, the way that leads to life. Amen.

Hunger

Ardith Baker

"The laborer's appetite works for him;
his hunger drives him on."
(Prov. 16:26)

IN SOLOMON's day, a physical hunger drove the laborers on, encouraging them to work hard so that they could earn a day's wages to buy food. In today's competitive world of business, other hungers—physical, mental, spiritual—drive us to labor long and hard:

> The hunger to get that raise;
> The hunger to close that deal;
> The hunger to get that promotion;
> The hunger to keep our job;
> The hunger to please our boss, client, or family;
> The hunger to make more money;
> The hunger to own our own business;
> The hunger to achieve;
> The hunger to move ahead;
> The hunger to succeed.

Hunger is a great motivator. However, it should not consume us to the point that nothing else matters. In Proverbs, God reminds us what we should really hunger for—wisdom from God. "How much better to get wisdom than gold, to choose understanding than silver!" (Prov. 16:16). When we seek God's wisdom and understanding first, we will see all of our *hungers* in a fresh perspective and we will be able to handle them appropriately. Why would we want it any other way?

Father, bless our efforts as we seek to fulfill our hunger and desire to know more about you. Guide us in this search and help us to apply all that we learn to our work and daily lives.

Body Language

Ardith Baker

"He who winks with his eye is plotting perversity;
he who purses his lips is bent on evil."

(Prov. 16:30)

You've seen it—someone makes a statement and then winks as if that covers up their true intentions. Or a person tells a lie while crossing their fingers behind their back. While this scripture is a warning against perversity and evil, it is interesting to note that a person's eyes and lips often give them away. God expects us to be discerning in order to know right from wrong and to avoid evil. One way to be discerning is to gain wisdom through studying the scriptures. Additionally, you can be discerning in everyday interactions with others by remaining cognizant of a person's body language. Body language speaks volumes about people and their intentions. The next time you go to a meeting, observe the people around you. Are they sitting up straight, making eye contact, perhaps taking notes or smiling? Or are they sitting slumped in the chair, avoiding eye contact, doodling, or text messaging? Based on their body language, which person would you want to work with on a project? Solomon gives us body language clues about the people that we should avoid—people with only evil intent on their minds. It doesn't require genius to discern someone's intentions based on body language; it requires that you be observant and consider a person's body language along with what he or she is saying or doing. Rely on God to guide you if you are still unsure, but do your part and be attentive to the clues.

Lord, help us to see beyond the obvious so that we may discern people's motives and understand the true meaning of things.

Games of Chance

ARDITH BAKER

"The lot is cast into the lap,
but its every decision is from the Lord."
(Prov. 16:33)

A N ARTICLE in *Fortune* relates a story of a company president using the game of Rock, Paper, Scissors to make a major business decision.[9] Unable to make the decision based on science or facts, he used a simple game of chance. Did he make the right decision? Only time will tell. Unfortunately, the company and stakeholders may suffer in the interim before the full extent of this outcome is determined. As shocking as this may seem, when you think about it, this most likely happens more often than we'd like to admit. Even when we base our decisions on logic, science, and facts, there is still an element of chance involved. By making assumptions and using mathematical formulas, decision theory models try to control this element of chance in the business world. However, decision models don't take into account one important factor—God. Proverbs tells us that our lives are not controlled by chance or fate. God is in control of everything. He is sovereign. We may toss a coin to help make a decision, but God knows and controls the outcome. Wouldn't you rather put your trust in God (a sure thing) than fate? Decision theory is important because it helps us make good sound judgments, and God expects us to use our knowledge. However, don't ever underestimate the power of prayer. Gather information and use

9. Jennifer Crick, "HAND JIVE," *Fortune* 151, no. 12 (2005): 40–42.

your knowledge, but always trust God. Seeking the guidance of the Sovereign God leads us to sound decisions.

Father, as we go through our day today, we take comfort in knowing that you are in control of every situation and that you are sovereign over all. Please do not let us make a bad decision, but help us serve you through wise choices.

A Man of Few Words

David Wesley Whitlock

"A man of knowledge uses words with restraint, and a man of understanding is even-tempered. Even a fool is thought wise if he keeps silent, and discerning if he holds his tongue."

(Prov. 17:27–28)

Serving as a board member for a local chamber of commerce years ago, I had the pleasure of serving with, and getting to know, Thomas Glenn Potter, the CEO of J. C. Potter's Sausage Company. He was a quiet man of few words, but he listened carefully during meetings. Several times, in the midst of some disagreement or discussion, I watched him as he would finally speak, and when he did, everyone listened. His words were always square on. Younger business professionals who had become quite animated and long-winded were often embarrassed (or should have been) at their bloviating and would have been more highly regarded had they just held their tongues. Plato is oft quoted as having said, "Wise men speak because they have something to say—fools because they have to say something." Many famous people—including Mark Twain, various U. S. presidents and others—are often credited with the quote, "It is better to keep your mouth shut and be thought a fool, than to speak and remove all doubt." But Plato and all the others were basically rephrasing what the scriptures teach in Proverbs 17. Thomas Glenn Potter was a man of few words. His example is worth following.

Father, make me a person of restraint, understanding, and even temper. "May the words of my mouth and the meditation of my heart be pleasing in your sight, O Lord, my Rock and my Redeemer" (Ps. 19:14).

A Simple Gift

ARDITH BAKER

"A gift opens the way for the giver and ushers him
into the presence of the great."

(Prov. 18:16)

I T'S THE little things in life that make a difference. Working late one night, I noticed him quietly moving from desk to desk, picking up the trash cans at each cubicle, and dumping them into the barrel he pulled behind him. Not a glorious or fashionable job, but an important one nonetheless. At my desk, he reached down and in one fluid movement dumped the trash and returned the can, all the while, being careful not to disturb me. "Thank you," I said. It caught him by surprise and caused him to pause ever so slightly. The look on his face said it all—pride at doing a good job and pleasure at being recognized for it. We give gifts for birthdays, anniversaries, Christmas, and almost every other occasion. Why can't we give gifts to our co-workers on a daily basis? Gifts such as a kind word, a smile, acknowledgement of a job well done, saying "please" and "thank you." These gifts do not require a tremendous sacrifice on our part, but the rewards are great. You'll notice that not only will the attitudes of your co-workers improve, but yours will too, resulting in a renewed spirit of cooperation. What an easy way to demonstrate your Christianity in the workplace! Your gift of kindness is a reflection of Christ's love for your co-workers. As we give these simple gifts and reflect Christ in our attitudes, we will truly be ushered into the presence of our Lord and be blessed!

Father, how easy it is to give a simple gift of a kind word. Help us to do so today. Place people in our paths who need encouragement so that we may share your Word with them.

Decision-Making

DAVID WESLEY WHITLOCK

*"Also it is not good for a soul to be without knowledge,
and he sins who hastens with his feet."*
(Prov. 19:2 NKJV)

RUSHING INTO a decision with insufficient information is dangerous and can lead to a bad decision and even into sin. Years ago, several acquaintances were purchasing stock in a local company; the outlook was good, and I made a decision to purchase shares. I prayed quickly that God would prevent me from purchasing the stock if I wasn't supposed to, but I launched ahead with little more thought. However, my broker wasn't able to meet me during lunch. Irritated, I went back to my office hungry, having spent all of my time in his waiting room. Several unsuccessful calls later, I determined to go back to his office. As I was leaving, a friend at work stopped me. "You shouldn't buy that stock," he said. I was stunned. "Why?" He answered, "I've been thinking about how you weren't sure whether you should own stock in a company that provides some products you aren't entirely comfortable with. . . ." I suddenly realized that *God* had been preventing me from buying the stock. Within the year, the stock had depreciated to junk status, and I would have lost money I really didn't have to invest in the first place, all because I attempted to make a decision without the right knowledge and motive. I was rushing headlong—hastening with my feet—to what would have been a devastating result. Be careful to get all the information you need before you rush into something you may regret.

*Help me to be patient, Lord, and make good decisions. I ask
for wisdom and know you give it liberally and without reproach.*

Integrity

JULIE HUNTLEY

"The righteous man walks in his integrity."
(Prov. 20:7a NKJV)

As GOD's children, we desire to be imitators of him. We know that his Word is his bond. As his children, we too should be men and women of integrity in all of our business dealings. We know that he "hastens" to perform his Word (Jer. 1:12) in our lives and does not alter the Word that has gone forth from his lips (Ps. 89:34). When we give our word, it should be as sure and binding as a legal contract. We must honor our word and not change what we have said—even when it doesn't seem to be in our best interest (Ps. 15:4). How can we expect God to honor his Word to us if we don't honor our word to others? So, too, should we place the highest esteem on the commitments we make to others. This, of course, includes time commitments. If you set an appointment, be there at the time you agreed. Marketing research has shown the importance of integrity in business relationships. When customers know they can rely on a sales representative's word, they will trust the sales person and be more committed to the relationship. Relationships characterized by greater levels of integrity, trust, and commitment lead to more profitable business outcomes. Isn't it great to see that research confirms what God has already told us? We continue to see the consistency between good business and biblical principles. Yes, the Bible can indeed be integrated into sound business practices.

Heavenly Father, in Jesus' name, I ask that you help me to keep my word in all of my business dealings. I ask that you show me when I've missed it. Please help me, one of your ambassadors, to demonstrate your character in all that I do. Thank you, Father, for loving me enough to correct me and strengthen me to do what is right in your sight.

Deception

Julie Huntley

"Bread gained by deceit is sweet to a man,
but afterward his mouth will be filled with gravel."
(Prov. 20:17 NKJV)

SATAN IS the father of lies. One of his greatest tools is deception (Rev. 12:9). Through deception, he can manipulate our
actions. Similarly, when used in business, deception is used to
manipulate and control the decisions and actions of people for
personal gain. Why would I want to deceive colleagues and act
as the child of a different father—the father of lies? Selfishness.
The root issue is one of motive. Am I being motivated by my
business colleague's and my customer's best interests—or by
my own selfish interest? While our motives may not be appar-
ent to others, we know God looks on the heart (1 Sam. 16:7).
Selfish motives lead to corrupt practices in business like deception. Truth in business allows others the freedom (John 8:32)
of making informed choices. While the profit from deception
initially offers a *sweet* sensation, like *gravel* in the mouth, it loses
its sweetness and even prevents the taste of sweetness in future
dealings. Imagine a mouth full of gravel! Not only would it be
difficult to enjoy the taste of anything, it would also become
very heavy in our mouths. So too, profit gained by deception
becomes burdensome, weighing very heavily on the heart. Profit
from honest practice leads to sweet victories and the satisfying
fulfillment that you have pleased your heavenly Father (Prov.
6:16–17) and not the father of deception.

Heavenly Father, in Jesus' name, I ask that you help me to discern when my motives are not pleasing to you. I determine to trust you to meet my needs as I meet the needs of others so that there is no need to practice deception. Please help me to experience the true sweetness of life as I live to honor you. Thank you, Father, for working in me that which brings pleasure to you.

Light from God

JULIE HUNTLEY

"The spirit of a man is the lamp of the Lord."
(Prov. 20:27a NKJV)

A KEY to success in business and any endeavor is receiving divine direction from the Lord. But, how does someone hear from God? While the Lord speaks through many sources, his Word often comes to us as a "quickened" word through our spirits. Whether it is a verse from the Bible or a comment from a friend, a word from the Lord comes alive to us through our spirit. There is the sensation of a light being turned on. Direction or understanding comes. This is because the spirit of a man is the "lamp" of the Lord. It is through our spirits that we receive light from the Lord. As children of God, we're supposed to be led by the Spirit of God (Rom. 8:14). The Holy Spirit brings light to our spirits (Rom. 8:16). Remember to acknowledge him (Prov. 3:6) when making business decisions. "Lord, should I sign this contract? Should I purchase this equipment through this vendor? What should I do in this situation?" Whatever the issue, check your spirit. Is there a sense of something not being right? Or do you sense a green light and peace? The Lord will help you to avoid a lot of pitfalls in business if you remember to look to him. He is the best counselor a business person could ever have. Remember to check your spirit for light.

Heavenly Father, I know you want me to succeed in my work. I desire to always do what is pleasing to you. I ask, in Jesus' name, for your heart in every decision I make. Please help me to discern between right and wrong in all of my choices. Thank you, Father, for your Holy Spirit guiding me in all that I do and showing me how to profit.

When You Get Where You're Going,
Where Will You Be?

DAVID WESLEY WHITLOCK

"All a man's ways seem right to him,
but the LORD weighs the heart."

(Prov. 21:2)

EVERY DAY we choose what path we will walk—which way we will go. We judge ourselves and others by the paths we choose. Yet God weighs the heart and knows our motivations. There is no hiding, justifying, or rationalizing before him. Years ago, I traveled with my supervisor to a conference in New Orleans. We drove ten minutes to an airport, were greeted by our flight crew, and boarded a private airplane. Our colleagues had driven nearly two hours in order to fly coach from Dallas-Fort Worth and then landed a long taxi ride from the hotel where our group had reservations. My boss and I landed, however, just minutes from downtown and were met by a stretch limousine. The driver dropped us off at the hotel, and my boss tipped him $20 and had our suitcases wheeled inside only to discover that we were at the wrong hotel. Frustrated and not wanting to spend any more money, he insisted we carry our own luggage and walk the two miles to the right hotel. Breaking in new boots with too many bags and in the humid heat of a New Orleans summer, I couldn't help thinking, *First class is no good if you don't arrive at the right location.* Another proverb reminds us, "There is a way that seems right to a man, but in the end it leads to death" (Prov. 14:12). When you get where you're going, do you know where you'll be?

Father, there is a way that seems right, but you know my heart. Keep me from the wrong way and lead me in your paths of righteousness so that I may be where you are.

Greedy for More or Anxious to Give?

David B. Whitlock

"They are always greedy for more,
while the godly love to give!"
(Prov. 21:26 NLT)

Y FRIEND Ernest Levingston is one of the most generous
givers I've ever met. He gives to various Christian causes
as the Holy Spirit guides him. But it wasn't always that way.
Ernest worked hard as he built his own engineering company,
succeeding very well financially. And although he gave to his local church, it was by no means a priority. Then through various
circumstances, Ernest lost most of what he had. He downsized
to a much smaller house, and the luxury automobile was exchanged for a pickup truck. However, through hard work and
perseverance, Ernest made a comeback. Now he gives the Lord
credit for his financial success. His trial by fire put matters into
perspective for Ernest. Giving was no longer an afterthought; it
became the joy of his life. That's why it's so easy for him to give
back to God; Ernest knows it is all from God anyway. Every
time I read Proverbs 21:26, I think of Ernest Levingston and am
encouraged by his example. Through his tribulation, he came to
understand that true happiness lies not in getting more but in
generous giving.

Lord, help me remember that you give me all I really need and
only ask for a giving heart in return. Open my heart that I may
open my wallet, my bank account, and all that I have for you.

First Maturity, Then Promotion

CHRIS PUTMAN

*"Humility and the fear of the Lord bring wealth
and honor and life."*

(Prov. 22:4)

I HAVE noticed that there is often a long wait before God promotes us to our dream—longer than we would chose for ourselves. Perhaps this is a maturing process he walks us through so that we don't get promoted prematurely. If we receive power and prosperity before we are spiritually and emotionally mature enough, the blessing can turn into a curse. If I desire that God place me into a position of influence over others, my motive needs to be pure. After all, "absolute power corrupts absolutely." Does my motive come from the desire to have my ego stroked, to make me feel important, or to lord over others? Or do I yearn for the position so that I can inspire and bless? Do I determine to gain respect, or do I instead look for opportunities to reach out to a worker who is discouraged? Do I enjoy intimidating others with my demanding nature, or will I develop sensitivity to others and become a servant leader? Do I also desire to be abundantly blessed financially? Is it for a lavish lifestyle to impress others? Or do I simply want my needs met so I can use the excess to water others, meet their needs, and spread the Gospel? I need to check my heart for the motive that drives that desire. Having the right motives—based on humility—is the first step toward fearing God and gaining wisdom so that he *can* bless us with wealth, honor, and life.

Father, please don't promote me beyond what my character can handle. I pray that you will open doors for me only when I am mature enough to manage the responsibility.

Core Values

Marshal H. Wright

"Train a child in the way he should go,
and when he is old he will not turn from it."

(Prov. 22:6)

IN *BUILT to Last: Successful Habits of Visionary Companies*, authors Collins and Porras assert that one of the most important attributes of highly successful companies is that they operate in accordance with a set of internal and enduring core values that provide essential stability in the face of ever-changing and competitive environments: "In a visionary company, the core values need no [market-based] rational or external justification. Nor do they sway with the trends and fads of the day. Nor even do they shift in response to changing market conditions."[10] In essence, these are the core values the organization is willing to die for. We—as Christian business leaders—need to train up and ground ourselves and our organizations in a set of enduring core values from which we will never turn regardless of the circumstances. We need to create and commit to a value system that we are willing to die for. If we don't, we are susceptible to being blown about by the winds of change. Now, what values are you grounded in that you are willing to die for? For me, the answer is that I need to be grounded in only those values that flow out of the Word, revelation, and grace of God. "For . . . the grass withers and the flowers fall, but the Word of the Lord stands forever" (1 Pet. 1:24). All

---

10. Jim Collins and Jerry I. Porras, *Built to Last: Successful Habits of Visionary Companies* (New York: HarperCollins Publishers, 1997).

other value systems are temporary and insufficient from an eternal perspective.

Lord, I pray that today your love and grace will flow over me and light my path so that I may be grounded in, and stay true to, your Word and revelation regardless of my surrounding circumstances. Thank you for revealing your presence and for being my rock and stability in the face of ever-changing times.

Balance Your Life

BRETT ANDREWS

*"Do not wear yourself out to get rich;
have the wisdom to show restraint."*

(Prov. 23:4)

HAVE YOU ever known someone who is driven by their internal desire and work ethic to continually achieve more
and more in his or her career? Solomon advises us to "have the
wisdom to show restraint" as we strive for career advancement.
Work, by itself, is not a bad thing. In fact, God ordained work
when he gave Adam work in the Garden of Eden. However, in
addition to the profession to which he has called us, God has
clearly outlined additional priorities that need care and feeding
throughout our lifetime. Worship, maintaining our relationships with God, caring for our families, and caring for God's
sheep—the widows, children, and poor—are all important
priorities in the Lord's eyes. Take a moment this week at work
and check your calendar. Are any of these additional priorities
present? Pray and ask the Lord's help in revealing the areas of
your life that need balance. He is faithful and will answer; giving you the necessary strength and insight to make changes that
please him.

*Lord, show me the areas in my life that need to be balanced.
Give me a heart for the priorities that you have ordained for me.
Give me a command of the tools (such as patience, time manage-
ment, and contentment) that I need to accomplish this.*

Uncompromising Commitment

JOSEPH J. BUCCI

"Don't steal the land of defenseless orphans by moving the ancient
boundary markers, for their Redeemer is strong. He himself will bring
their charges against you. Commit yourself to instruction;
attune your ears to hear words of knowledge."

(Prov. 23:10–12 NLT)

EVEN WITH the exposure of ethical violations by the leaders of
major corporations, greater scrutiny of the SEC, laws such
as Sarbanes-Oxley, and the booming business being handled by
compliance officers and accounting audits[11], ethics continues to
be debated and skirting the law is still an inherent part of many a
business environment. A recent survey noted that 56 percent of
employees who participated in the research had observed violations of ethics standards, policies, or the law; yet 42 percent of
those who witnessed misconduct did not report it.[12] Having a
code of ethics on a company's wall or an 800-number available
to employees for reporting violations of ethical standards are important safeguards. But people of faith must live by an inner code
written on their hearts. Many verses in Proverbs offer practical
advice and warnings to those who would harm the poor or needy
children of our heavenly Father. Here, perhaps, the most insight-
ful verse is not the command to avoid deception or cheating nor

11. B. L. Ochman, *EthicsCrisis.com* (2006, August 17) Retrieved
December 18, 2007, from http://ethicscrisis.com/blog_posts/ethics
_compliance/.

12. J. Kim, ed. "Has Sarbox really changed attitudes?" *FierceSarbox.
com* (2007, December 4) Retrieved December 18, 2007, from http://www
.fiercesarbox.com/story/has-sarbox-really-changed-attitudes/2007-12-04.

the threat of the retribution by the redeemer, but rather the command enjoining us all to continue to grow in knowledge. Many famous leaders in both religious and business environments found themselves in compromising situations when they lost sight of accountability. Be willing to learn and grow. Develop your skills and maximize your talents through instruction and training. But do not neglect to sow seeds of instruction into the fertile soil of your heart.

May my heart continue to be sensitive to your Word, and open to your instruction. Plant good seed in the soil of my heart, and guide my steps to live rightly and honor you by my words and deeds.

Instruction and Knowledge

ARDITH BAKER

*"Apply your heart to instruction
and your ears to words of knowledge."*

(Prov. 23:12)

As a business person, you need to stay current on trends and other issues specific to your trade. In order to do so, you have to receive instruction and "words of knowledge." How will you receive this instruction? From where will the words of knowledge come? From whom will you learn? In addition to family and friends, your choices in the business arena include employers, co-workers, competitors, clients, trainers, consultants, and other experts who have been successful. In fact, each person who crosses your path on a daily basis acts as a mentor of sort, providing you with vast amounts of words of knowledge. With so much information, how do you know which words to apply? How are you able to discern the good from the bad and the dangerous? The most important word of knowledge comes from God through his scriptures. By studying God's Word and applying his instruction to your personal and business lives, you will be able to discern the good and bad in worldly "knowledge." This is an ongoing battle as trends, ideas, and problems in the business world are ever changing, requiring you to constantly acquire more information and words of knowledge. Fortunately, God's Word never changes. Therefore, if you apply yourself to the instruction of God through his Word, you will be able to weed out the wise instruction from the bad in order to obtain words of knowledge that will help you and your business succeed.

Thank you for the gift of your written Word, Lord. Help me to fully absorb its meaning so that I will understand words of knowledge that will guide and direct my thoughts and actions. Help me to apply the words of knowledge to my business so that it will succeed and give you glory.

Hope

Ardith Baker

*"There is surely a future hope for you,
and your hope will not be cut off."*
(Prov. 23:18)

IN THIS day and age, many people lose hope and for many reasons. Layoffs, age discrimination, no retirement, no health care, buy-outs—the reasons abound. Uncertainty seems to follow us day to day, and yet we continue to hope. Where do you place your hope? Perhaps in your job, your abilities, your spouse, the stock market, or your 4019(k)? All of these have the potential to fail us, so why do we not panic? Why don't we give up and drop out of society to wander aimlessly through life? Some people do, but as Christians, we keep moving forward, driven to a higher purpose, trusting with a faith that makes us persevere when all else seems futile. We do so because we put our hope in God! We trust him to take care of us even when all else fails. Even when our job is gone, our finances disappear, or we lose our health insurance, we place our hope in God to see us through the trials. As believers in Christ, we have his promise to help us through the good times and the bad. Take comfort in his Word: "in all things God works for the good of those who love him, who have been called according to his purpose" (Rom. 8:28). With our hope appropriately placed in God, we will be beacons of light to those without hope, drawing them to the Lord and, in turn, giving them hope for a better life.

Dear Heavenly Father, please use me today to show your unfailing love to a dark and hurting world without hope. Amen.

Strategic Planning

Marshal H. Wright

*"By wisdom a house is built, and through understanding
it is established; through knowledge its rooms are filled
with rare and beautiful treasures."*

(Prov. 24:3–4)

THE STRATEGIC planning process has been described as "a
careful diagnosis of an organization's current conditions (as
manifested by its external and internal environments) so that appropriate strategic actions can be recommended."[13] Obviously,
the ability to conduct "careful diagnosis" and recommend "appropriate strategic action" requires the presence of wisdom,
understanding, and knowledge. This proverb aptly describes the
results of strategic planning efforts that are applied by leaders
gifted with these attributes. Their organizations are "built," "established," and blessed to prosper beyond measure, so indicated
by their being "filled with rare and beautiful treasures." How is
your organization doing in the strategic planning process? Is the
organization being built up and established to its full potential?
Is it prospering? Seek the Lord daily and ask him for supernatural
wisdom, understanding, and knowledge so that you can better
lead your organization successfully forward through the critical
and very important strategic planning processes.

13. Michael A. Hitt, R. Duane Ireland, and Robert E. Hoskisson,
Strategic Management: Competitiveness and Globalization, 5th ed. (Cincinnati: South-Western College Publishing, 2003), C.i.

Lord, I pray that as I seek you, that you—through the power of the Holy Spirit—will empower me with supernatural wisdom, understanding, and knowledge so that I can contribute more and help my organization move forward in a strategic and Godly manner.

Seeking Success

Ardith Baker

"It is the glory of God to conceal a matter;
to search out a matter is the glory of kings."
(Prov. 25:2)

Have you ever played the childhood game of "Hide and Seek" where one child hides while others seek her out? The pleasure is in seeking all the hiding places until the hidden playmate is found. Success in business is similar to this game of "Hide and Seek." God wants us to be successful and yet we often have to seek it out. Like the game, we often look in the wrong places and are unsuccessful in achieving our goal. However, God gives us the grace to persevere. We continue to seek through hardships and trials, through endurance, and sometimes pain. Being a Christian does not exclude us from failure. In fact, successful businesspeople know that it is often the failures that lead them to success. By placing our trust in God, the failures make us stronger, wiser, and motivate us to work harder to achieve success. Through God, Christians allow failure to refine and perhaps redirect but never to stop us. Solomon reminds us, "[F]or though a righteous man falls seven times, he rises again, but the wicked are brought down by calamity" (Prov. 24:16). Don't give up. Seek God's will in your life. If you trust him to guide and direct you, even through the failures, you will be assured that your success was earned and well deserved.

Father, thank you for your grace that helps me persevere through the trials. Help me to put my trust in you and learn from my failures so that I will ultimately succeed and glorify your name.

Timing

Chris Putman

"Timely advice is as lovely as golden apples
in a silver basket."
(Prov. 25:11 TLB)

SQUIRMING IMPATIENTLY at my school desk as a young girl, I'd bolt at the sound of the recess bell. Running into the schoolyard, my friends and I would snatch up a ragged piece of twine and jump rope with passion. I loved it because I had the endurance to jump almost indefinitely as my friends stood by and counted my repetitions. I held the record. Then my skill was challenged when someone introduced Double Dutch, performed by jumping inside two ropes rotating in opposite directions. As they beat in rhythm, I'd wait outside the ropes for the right time to dive in and jump, but I never got past the obstacle of jumping in because I couldn't get the timing right. Even now in life, I still wrestle with timing. Often, when God reveals a management breakthrough to me I explode with the enthusiasm of having the solution and want to dive right in. But in doing so, I make a mess of my circumstances and offend my boss, co-workers, or employees by using God's gift too soon. Although equipped with what I need for the challenge, I get the timing wrong. Moving forward too soon, I'm not received well. Waiting too long, I miss an open door. It takes a sensitive ear to hear God's timing for life's path.

God, help us to tune into your rhythm, to hear that delicate beat so that we have the wisdom to know when the time is right to jump in.

Aptly Spoken Words

Ardith Baker

"A word aptly spoken is like apples of gold in settings of silver."
(Prov. 25:11)

CERTAINLY YOU can recall a time when harsh words were spoken to you. It takes only one harsh or thoughtless word to penetrate the soul like a knife. The resulting spiritual wound can take up to a lifetime to heal. Conversely, words can be used to heal, soothe, and uplift. However, like a healing salve, these words need to be reapplied frequently. How will you use your words today? Very often in business situations, you must think quickly, reacting to the immediate situation or crisis facing you. In times like these, often the first words that come to mind (out of frustration, anger, or fear) are harsh words. It is so easy to use harsh words to express our emotions, to rebuke, correct, or discipline employees or co-workers. And yet, do we achieve the desired result? More often, we simply crush the spirit of those we address. Before you begin your work day, major project, business meeting, phone call, or e-mail, ask God to give you the appropriate words to speak: aptly spoken words that make a point without wounding the soul; words of wisdom and instruction, not destruction; words that uplift and encourage, not discourage. Not only will you be a better businessperson, but you will also reflect the glorious God that we serve, a loving and kind God whose written Word is "like apples of gold in settings of silver." How will you use your words today?

Lord, today I want to use my words to encourage, instruct, and lift up those around me. Help me to choose my words carefully so that I may express your enduring love for humankind.

Fire Prevention

*"For lack of wood the fire goes out, and where there is no whisperer,
contention quiets down. Like charcoal to hot embers
and wood to fire, so is a contentious man to kindle strife."*
(Prov. 26:20–21 NAS)

A FIRE of any type requires three elements: fuel, oxygen, and a spark. Removal of any one of these elements keeps a fire from starting or extinguishes a fire once begun. Fire fighting is all about removing one or more of these elements through water, foam, and other means. Most workplaces have smoke detectors and sprinkler systems to extinguish a fire quickly. Another kind of fire that often goes undetected in workplaces is what Proverbs refers to as the smoldering, underlying contention that kindles strife and demeans, divides, and discourages community. James speaks of the tongue as a fire: "See, how great a forest is set aflame by such a small fire" (James 3:5 NAS). The root cause of contention is selfishness—we seek to put down others in order to make ourselves seem better or smarter or more just. While fire destroys physical structures which can often be rebuilt or re-placed, contention destroys something far less replaceable—trust and respect. Are you a fire preventer or a fire starter? Do you seek to build others up, or put them down? Are you more likely to be a source of encouragement or a source of contention?

Lord, give us wisdom and grace to be quick to hear that which builds and heals and slow to speak that which damages and divides.

Avoid Gossip

Ardith Baker

*"The words of a gossip are like choice morsels;
they go down to a man's inmost parts."*
(Prov. 26:22)

DID YOU hear what happened upstairs? Do you know about the changes taking place? Can you believe what is going on? Gossip occurs frequently in the workplace. Everyone wants the latest information, and sometimes the easiest way to get it is from the grapevine. However, this information is often exaggerated, biased, and inaccurate and can lead to misunderstandings or worse. Information is power, so people with even a little bit of information, whether accurate or inaccurate, will relish that feeling of power when they pass it on. But gossip is often used to harm others and to wage emotional wars behind the scenes. Reputations can be severely damaged from gossip. The best thing you can do to stop gossip is to not pass it on. Solomon says, "Without wood a fire goes out; without gossip a quarrel dies down" (Prov. 26:20). By refusing to pass along gossip, you help *put the fire out* and stop the quarrel. Consider Paul's description of those deserving God's wrath:

> They have become filled with every kind of wickedness, evil, greed and depravity. They are full of envy, murder, strife, deceit and malice. They are gossips, slanderers, God-haters, insolent, arrogant and boastful; they invent ways of doing evil; they disobey their parents; they are senseless, faithless, heartless, ruthless (Rom. 1:29–31).

Wow, amidst the God-haters, evil, greedy, and depraved are gossips. Avoid gossip; otherwise, the reputation that may be hurt may be yours. Be discerning with the information you hear and don't spread untruths.

Lord, I want to exemplify you. Please help me to guard my words today. Use my words to encourage those around me, not to bring others down. Amen.

Marketing Ourselves

Edward W. Walton

Do not boast about tomorrow,
for you do not know what a day may bring forth.

(Prov. 27:1 NIV)

WHAT IS the difference between boasting and marketing yourself or your project or your company? We are taught that we must *market* ourselves to move up the corporate ladder or to get our project off the ground or to get the recognition we *deserve*. However, our Lord gives us a different model—one that requires humility and patience, traits that few of us possess. While many of us desire these traits, most of us have a hard time exercising them. The Lord gave us a sterling example of humility and patience that led to delayed recognition. As creator of the universe, Jesus laid aside his position in glory, humbly and patiently suffered for us, and the Father exalted him in due time (Phil. 2:5–11). When we follow his example, we are promised the same result (James 4:10). How do we market ourselves without boasting? We recognize the efforts of others, such as our team, or we recognize the benefit our project or company will be to the lives of others. As for boasting about ourselves, we follow the advice given in Proverbs 27:2 to let others boast about us, keep our mouths closed, exercise patience and humility, and watch the Lord accomplish his work in our lives.

Lord, help me to exercise humility and patience and recognize the accomplishments of those around me. Help me to accomplish the tasks you set before me without a desire for recognition reflective of a boastful heart.

Warning Signs

Ardith Baker

*"The prudent see danger and take refuge,
but the simple keep going and suffer for it."*
(Prov. 27:12)

IT WAS a beautiful summer evening when I began my two-hour drive home. I enjoyed the countryside and watched the clouds build in the sky ahead of me as I drove. I watched as the clouds formed majestic crowns through which the evening sunset shone. Farther on, the once peaceful clouds became ominous. The wind blew, rain fell, and lightening flashed all around. Still I drove on. With each lightening flash I anxiously looked up at the darkening sky and watched in horror as thin tendrils of cloud threatened to touch the ground. Despite the fact that the road was barely visible, I still drove on. I could see the warning signs all around me, a dangerous situation was ahead, and yet I ignored the signs and my swelling fear, and drove on. Sometimes subtle, sometimes direct, God provides warning signs to save us from dangerous situations. What are the warning signs in business? They vary from situation to situation and person to person, so you need to keep your eyes open and observe. Be prudent, discerning, and prayerful so that you will not only recognize warning signs, but allow them to change your path so that you won't drive into danger. If you do drive into the storm, with God's help you may make it through unscathed as I did (although my two-hour drive became a terrifying four-hour drive); but you may not. Don't take that chance. Watch for God's warning signs and follow them to safety.

Thank you, Lord, for loving me so much that you would place warning signs in my path to keep me from danger. Help me not only to recognize the warning signs, but provide me with wisdom and courage to heed them. Amen.

Refining Each Other

Ardith Baker

"As iron sharpens iron, so one man sharpens another."
(Prov. 27:17)

Hey, can I bounce this idea off of you? Can I run something by you? What do you think of this? Why don't we try . . . ? When we ask our co-workers or bosses to consider our ideas, we are looking for acceptance and constructive criticism that will help us grow and sharpen our skills. So, don't be offended if their response is less than favorable. Solomon said that we sharpen each other, but sometimes the edge cuts into our pride. How else will we learn and refine our skills unless we take a chance and share our ideas? Whether a response is favorable or unfavorable, prayerfully consider the advice given, ponder it, pray about it, and ask God to open your eyes so that you can improve your idea or project. By doing this, you will put your pride behind you and will grow not only in knowledge and skill but also in esteem. You will be able to bounce back quickly with even greater ideas and contributions. Then, having gone through the refining process yourself, when others ask you what you think about their ideas, you will be sensitive, considerate, and able to provide good constructive criticism to help refine them.

Father, as I go through the refining process, please help me to be humble and not to take offense. Help me to be open and willing to learn from my mentors so that I may improve and grow. In return, help me to be a good mentor to those you send my way. Amen.

A Heart's Reflection

Ardith Baker

*"As water reflects a face,
so a man's heart reflects the man."*
(Prov. 27:19)

YOUR ACTIONS and decisions are a reflection of what you hold dear in your heart. You only have to observe someone for a short amount of time in order to discern their motives for doing things. What do people observe about you? What do you hold dear in your heart? Examine yourself to see if you are holding God dear in your heart. If you do, your actions and decisions will be based on God rather than on the world. People will notice there is something different—better—about you, and your life will be a tremendous witness for God. Now, what about in your workplace? Do you go through your day so caught up in business issues, turmoil, and decisions that you forget what your reflection looks like? Do your co-workers, supervisors, managers, clients, or customers look at you and see God's reflection in your attitude and decisions, or do they merely see an ordinary man or woman? Stop for a moment and reflect. Close your eyes, take a deep breath, and feel your heart beat. Smile and know that God counts each beat and lovingly and tenderly holds you in the palm of his hand. With God's help

> You *can* excel at your work;
> You *can* make the right decision;
> You *can* make the presentation;
> You *can* meet the deadline;
> You *can!*

When you hold God dear in your heart, your reflection will be beautiful, confident, and complete, able to meet any challenge that comes your way.

Lord, I want to be a reflection of you. Please cleanse my heart today and fill me with your presence and peace. Amen.

Know the State of Your Flocks

DAVID WESLEY WHITLOCK

"Be diligent to know the state of your flocks,
and attend to your herds."

(Prov. 27:23 NKJV)

FOR MOST young men growing up in rural Oklahoma several decades ago, enrollment in vocational agriculture courses and membership in the local Future Farmers of America (FFA) chapter were fairly standard. For my FFA projects, I raised lambs, goats, pigs, and a small bevy of rabbits, chickens, and even 200 parakeets at one point. But of all the animals I raised, sheep required the greatest attention and care. Constant attention to their condition was critical. No wonder the writer of this proverb stressed the need to know the state of one's flocks and attend to them. This wisdom is true for the people God has entrusted to your care as well. Many times, misunderstandings, miscommunications, and frustrations in the workplace are simply the result of managers or supervisors being oblivious to the personal struggles of their employees. It is much easier to remain ignorant and detached from those with whom we work as opposed to investing our time and interest in their lives. Do you care for your employees and subordinates as if they were charges for you to keep? Do you approach your position of authority with an attention to your followers' condition? Are you so concerned with your own welfare or with the things of work that you have forgotten the most important asset of all—your people? Do you know the state of your flocks; are you attending to their needs?

In the midst of the urgent demands of work, Father, help me see those you have entrusted to my supervision through your eyes. Give me discernment in knowing their condition and help me to attend to their needs.

Usury

David Wesley Whitlock

*"He who increases his wealth by exorbitant interest
amasses it for another, who will be kind to the poor."*

(Prov. 28:8)

THE BIBLE condemns lending money at exorbitant interest—usury, and Psalm 15 carries the prohibition against
usury. The principle taught seems predominately centered on
not charging interest to *brothers* but rather giving to them (and
especially to the poor) what is needed without interest.[14] "Do
not charge your brother interest, whether on money or food or
anything else that may earn interest" (Deut. 23:19). However,
the prohibition of interest does not seem to hold when dealing with those outside the family of faith: "You may charge a
foreigner interest, but not a brother Israelite . . ." (Deut. 23:20).
Even then, though, usury is prohibited. For example, "Do not
mistreat an alien or oppress him . . ." (Exod. 22:21). In a parable
in Matthew, Christ taught that the miserly servant who buried
his talent should have instead put his master's money on deposit
with bankers so that at the least the master would have earned
interest (Matt. 25). Jesus taught his followers, "Give to the one
who asks you, and don't turn away from the one who wants to
borrow from you" (Matt. 5:42). Neither lending nor borrowing

14. These principles are intended primarily for individual believers in
personal practice. They may not apply to banks or mortgage companies
in which a person is responsible for granting loans. In such cases, a
Christian is investing others' money and representing others' interests.
Christians must seek the leading of the Holy Spirit regarding their
personal involvement in lending and borrowing.

is specifically condemned in the Bible, yet under no circumstance should the interest be outside of normal, accepted rates. Usury is prohibited in the practice of all lending situations.

Make me into a person who freely gives and is generous to the poor and to my fellow believers. May you never allow me to engage in usury, be selfish, or turn a blind eye to the needs of others.

Discernment

Ardith Baker

*"If a ruler listens to lies,
all his officials become wicked."*

(Prov. 29:12)

HOW INTERESTING. Solomon knew that if a ruler (CEO, CFO, CIO, president, vice president, manager, supervisor, coordinator) listened to lies, all his or her officials (everyone reporting to him/her and on down the corporate ladder) would become wicked, perpetuating these lies and pervading the corporate culture. Entertaining lies, half truths, exaggerated, or inaccurate information can only lead to more inaccuracies. Imagine building a business on this type of foundation where employees are afraid to tell the truth or perhaps the "rulers" don't want to hear it. Perhaps you did not establish this practice but are now caught up in it. Regardless of the situation, no business can thrive for very long on this type of management style. It may seem like the company is prospering, but eventually the lies cause the foundation to crumble and collapse, leaving the business in shambles, your career ruined, or both. How can you guard against lies and not get caught up in the process? Ask God for discernment and then rely on him to help you make sound judgments. Through discernment, you will be able to recognize the truth from the lies, the accurate from the inaccurate, and you will hold yourself and others accountable to the truth. Once you take a stand for truth, no matter what the cost, God will honor your decision and will bless you and your business dealings. Don't be afraid to take a stand, discern the truth, and establish a sound business foundation.

Lord, help me to be a person of integrity today. Use me to be an example of truth and honesty to those with whom I work. Amen.

Teamwork

Ardith Baker

*"Where there is no revelation, the people cast off restraint;
but blessed is he who keeps the law."*

(Prov. 29:18)

As a small child, I would pull out a board game, wanting to play. But, unable to read the instructions, I made up my own rules. Not surprisingly, no one wanted to play with me because I would change the rules to suit me as the game progressed. As business managers, we need to clearly state the *rules of the game* at the beginning of the project and then stick to them. Make sure everyone on your team knows and understands the rules and your expectations so there won't be any misunderstanding or miscommunication. Nothing causes frustration faster than even the slightest perception of changing rules in the middle of the game. The last thing you want is for a few of your team members to start making up their own rules because they don't understand what you expect from them. As a team, you should function cohesively, working together effectively to achieve a common goal. This can only be done if you, as the manager and team leader, let everyone know from the beginning what is expected. Then, hold your team to that task. Monitor your project and team members carefully to make sure everyone stays on task. We all have to adapt to changing conditions, especially in business, but unless situations change, don't change the rules midstream. Be consistent, be fair, and be an example. Guide and direct your team to success, and in the end, the entire team will be blessed.

Lord, help me, as part of a team, to lead fairly or follow justly. I pray that you will give me wisdom and the ability to serve you no matter what my role may be so that I will be a blessing to my team.

Fighting Fear

Ardith Baker

*"Fear of man will prove to be a snare,
but whoever trusts in the Lord is kept safe."*

(Prov. 29:25)

I T WAS just an ordinary day that turned out to be anything but ordinary. After returning home from work, I parked my car in the garage as usual and headed inside. I rounded the corner into the front room and immediately stopped. Something was definitely out of the ordinary. The front door was wide open with splintered wood everywhere. Flooded with emotions, fear overcame me. What was missing? Was someone still in the house? Would I ever feel safe in my own home again? After all, a deadbolted door did nothing to stop the thieves. As I examined my home, I began to realize how God had protected me and my family and how much worse it could have been. So, I had a choice. I could be afraid of man and live in fear, or I could trust in God to continue to protect me. Put your trust in God so that your fears will not immobilize you. Similarly, in business, you cannot allow your actions to be based on your fears—such as fear of failure, fear of losing your job, or fear of the unknown. Allow yourself to be guided by your trust in God and his ability to protect and direct you through any situation that you face, whether you're at work or at home. After all, God did not give you a spirit of fear, but of power, and of love, and of a sound mind (2 Tim. 1:7 NKJV).

Jehovah-Shalom, the God of Peace; replace my fears and uncertainty with peace and teach me to walk in boldness through my trust in you. Thank you for your continual protection and direction.

Satisfaction Guaranteed

Ardith Baker

"[G]ive me neither poverty nor riches,
but give me only my daily bread.
Otherwise, I may have too much and disown you and say,
Who is the Lord?' Or I may become poor and steal,
and so dishonor the name of my God."

(Prov. 30:8b–9)

IN ONE of my favorite prints, artist Mary Englebreit shows a young girl enjoying a relaxing moment in a chair surrounded by all of her stuff. The caption reads "Princess of Quite-a-Lot."[15] I sometimes visualize myself in that chair as I look around my office and realize that I have *quite-a-lot* of stuff! It seems that the more stuff we accumulate, the more stuff we want: more clothes, a faster computer, a company car, a corporate expense account, that corner office with the window, more employees, more clients, more money, more, more, more. What I really want is to just be satisfied with what I have. This is an important stewardship principle. Before God will give you more, you should be satisfied with and a good steward of what he has already given you. The writer of this proverb recognized that if he had too much, he would place too much importance on himself and become dissatisfied with his life. If he had too little, he would place too much emphasis on himself and become dissatisfied with his life. Satisfaction in life comes only from placing importance and emphasis on God and allowing him to drive our ambition and

15. Mary Englebreit, Inc. © ME, Inc. 2002 Retrieved December 20, 2007 from http://shop.maryengelbreit.com/detail.aspx?ID=4329.

provide for our needs. It's an amazing thing, though, that once we depend on God to provide for all our needs and are satisfied with what he has given to us, he will entrust us as his stewards with even more.

Jehovah-jireh, God the Provider, thank you for all that you have given me. Thank you for providing for all my needs; I am blessed beyond measure. Help me to be a good steward today by sharing your blessings with others in need.

The Proverbs 31 Manager

Ardith Baker

*"She watches over the affairs of her household and does not eat the
bread of idleness. Her children arise and call her blessed;
her husband also, and he praises her: . . . Give her the reward
she has earned, and let her works bring her praise at the city gate."*

(Prov. 31:27–28, 31)

VERSES 10-31 of Proverbs 31 describe the quintessential woman—one that all women should emulate. But let's view these scriptures from a business perspective and apply it to man and woman alike. The Proverbs 31 woman described here is an amazing example of management at its best. Not only is she a multi-tasker, but she also cares for and nurtures her employees. She is gracious to offer help to her co-workers and employees when needed. She is not afraid to put in the necessary time to get the job done or even to do the work herself. She stays abreast of current trends so as to help her company remain profitable. She is a source of information and encouragement for all. Her noble character, leadership skills, and good works earn her an excellent reputation and respect among her peers, which greatly benefits her company as well. Her *CEO* has complete confidence in her abilities. She is the manager that we should all strive to be. How does she do all this, and how can we be more like her? She does it because she maintains her focus on God, and, yes, with God's help we can do it too. With God as our focus and his written Word as our guide and example, we can greatly improve our management skills. We can be the Proverbs 31 manager!

Father, help me today to be a Proverbs 31 manager—not for my glory but for yours. Show me where I need to improve as I go through my day. Show me how to improve as I read your Word. Help me to maintain my focus on you through all the distractions. Amen.

Epilogue: Our Prayer

THE CALLING to work in the field of business is a challenge, especially for the devoted believer. Christians who are called to minister in the marketplace have a great potential to make an eternal impact for the Kingdom. They also have a tremendous potential for harm to the cause of Christ. For many years now, I have become increasingly convinced that our world—and the marketplace especially—is sorely in need of winsome witnesses. While it is critical that we share the gospel of Jesus Christ in word, and while we know the Word says that Christ is a stumbling block and offense to many, as witnesses of his grace we need not add to the offense. I believe it is possible, imperative even, that as believers and partakers of the grace of God, we are called to be gentle in our persuading—uncompromising, yet winsome and motivated by love.

Our prayer with this small volume of devotions is that you apply God's Word, his wisdom, and his instruction to your life, both personally and professionally. *Lead like Jesus*, as the title of a recent book by Ken Blanchard and Phil Hodges encourages. If you are a Christian business professional reading this book, develop the habit my co-editor encouraged in the *Introduction*. Read the Proverbs daily. But don't settle for that; read the whole of God's Word and pray that God use your time in Bible study to develop a closer walk and more intimate relationship with him. Yours is a noble calling. God has great things in store for you as you seek daily to serve him, glorify him, and serve others in the marketplace. Others are watching, observing, and forming opinions about the one in whom you say you've placed your trust. What a tremendous responsibility. Your only hope of success—the only success that really matters—is to rely on Jesus.

Father, in the name of Jesus, our Lord and Savior, mold us into the image of your Son. Teach us. Lead us. Give us wisdom and discernment. Help us to live a life that glorifies you in our personal lives and in our professions. Help us become uncompromising in integrity, bold in our witness, but all the while loving, gentle, and winsome. Amen.

—David Wesley Whitlock

Bibliography

Collins, Jim. *Good to Great*. New York: HarperCollins Publishers, Inc., 2001.

Collins, Jim, and Jerry I. Porras. *Built to Last: Successful Habits of Visionary Companies*. New York: HarperCollins Publishers, 1997.

Crick, Jennifer. "HAND JIVE." *Fortune* 151, no. 12 (2005): 40–42.

Daft, Richard L., *Organization Theory and Design*, 7th ed. Cincinnati: South-Western College Publishing, 2001.

Hitt, Michael A., R. Duane Ireland, and Robert E. Hoskisson. *Strategic Management: Competitiveness and Globalization*, 5th ed. Cincinnati: South-Western College Publishing, 2003.

Huang, Yi-hui. "OPRA: A Cross-Cultural, Multiple-Item Scale for Measuring Organization—Public Relationships." *Journal of Public Relations Research* 13, no. 1 (2001): 61–90.

Kim, J. ed. "Has Sarbox really changed attitudes?" *FierceSarbox. com* (2007, December 4). Retrieved December 18, 2007, from http://www.fiercesarbox.com/story/has-sarbox-really-changed -attitudes/2007-12-04.

Mary Englebreit, Inc. © ME, Inc. 2002 Retrieved December 20, 2007 from http://shop.maryengelbreit.com/detail.aspx?ID=4329.

Milkovich, George T., and Jerry Newman. *Compensation*. New York: McGraw-Hill/Irwin, 2005.

Noe, Raymond Andrew, John R. Hollenbeck, Barry Gerhart, and Patrick Wright. *Fundamentals of Human Resource Management*, 2nd ed. New York: McGraw-Hill/Irwin, 2007.

Ochman, B. L. *EthicsCrisis.com* (2006, August 17). Retrieved December 18, 2007, from http://ethicscrisis.com/blog_posts/ethics_compliance/.

Schein, Edgar H. *Organizational Culture and Leadership*, 2nd ed. San Francisco: Jossey-Bass Publishers, 1992.

Contributing Authors

Brett Andrews
> Vice President for Adult and Graduate Studies
> Oklahoma Wesleyan University

Ardith Baker
> Assistant Professor of Business
> Oral Roberts University School of Business

Joseph J. Bucci
> Assistant Professor of Business
> Geneva College

Timothy DeClue
> Chair and Professor of Computer and Information Sciences
> Southwest Baptist University

David Dyson
> Professor of Management
> Oral Roberts University School of Business

Vickie Shamp Ellis
> Associate Professor of Communication Arts
> Oklahoma Baptist University

Julie Huntley
> Professor of Marketing
> Oral Roberts University School of Business

Contributing Authors

Sharon Johnson
> Director of Graduate Programs, Director of Institutional Research,
> and Professor of Management
> Cedarville University

Bob Klostermeyer
> Chair and Associate Professor of Political Science and History
> Southwest Baptist University

Phillip V. Lewis
> Dean of the College of Professional Studies
> Oklahoma Christian University

Susan Lynch
> Chair and Professor of Business Administration
> Southwest Baptist University

Walter MacMillan
> Professor of Management
> Oral Roberts University School of Business

Chris Putman
> Instructor of Journalism
> Oral Roberts University School of Arts and Cultural Studies

Tim Redmer
> Professor of Accounting
> Regent University

Rich Rudebock
> Dean of the Paul Dickenson School of Business
> Oklahoma Baptist University

Gil Trout
> Chairman and CEO
> South Central Region, UMB Bank

Edward W. Walton
> Dean of Libraries
> Southwest Baptist University

Darin W. White
> Director of Research and Professor of Marketing of the McAfee
> School of Business
> Union University

David B. Whitlock
> Pastor, Lebanon Baptist Church, Lebanon, Kentucky
> Adjunct Faculty, Campbellsville University

David Wesley Whitlock
> Associate Provost and Dean of the College of Business and
> Computer Science
> Southwest Baptist University

Marshal H. Wright
> Interim Dean and Professor of Business
> Oral Roberts University School of Business

Author Index

Scripture Index